The Captives of Abb's Valley

RESIDENCE OF CAPTAIN MOORE—"IT WAS A QUIET SECLUDED SPOT, THE VERY PARADISE OF THE HUNTER AND GRAZIER."

The Captives of Abb's Valley

The Massacre & Captivity of Settlers in Virginia by Indians, 1786

James Moore

A Son of Mary Moore

LEONAUR

The Captives of Abb's Valley
The Massacre & Captivity of Settlers in Virginia by Indians, 1786
by James Moore
A Son of Mary Moore

First published under the title
The Captives of Abb's Valley

Leonaur is an imprint of Oakpast Ltd

Copyright in this form © 2012 Oakpast Ltd

ISBN: 978-1-78282-040-6 (hardcover)
ISBN: 978-1-78282-041-3 (softcover)

http://www.leonaur.com

Contents

Introduction

"*Truth is stranger than fiction.*" This remark has been often repeated, and the history of the world teems with incidents that show its correctness. The press of the present day throws off numberless works of fiction different in their character, and suited to the various tastes of those who read. In this little volume there is no fiction. An attempt has been made to gather and arrange the incidents in the lives of a few individuals who were actors in scenes of no common kind. It is a matter of regret that more efforts of the same kind have not been made. In many sections of our country, occurrences rich in interest have been lost hopelessly, by the death of the last of those in whose memories they were treasured.

In various ways, imperfect sketches of this tale have been given to the public. The attempt to give it in a more complete form than any in which it has appeared heretofore, has been made at the earnest suggestion of those in whose judgment the writer places much confidence; and with the hope that it will form neither an unentertaining, nor a useless addition to the many little volumes issuing from the press. No pains have been spared to make the narrative accurate; and while it is believed that all the leading incidents have been given, it is at the same time well known that many of the details which would have added no little to the interest of the work, have now passed beyond the reach of recall.

My mother never gave a detailed narrative to any person; but on the contrary always showed a disinclination to converse on the subject. Two attempts were made to secure such a relation from her. The first was by my father some months after their marriage. The effort soon brought on her such a paroxysm of grief, that it was abandoned; and never again attempted by him. The other was made by her oldest son during her last illness; and he soon saw that it was exciting her feelings so much, that he dropped the subject. Those who follow her through the scenes related in the following pages, will not be surprised that her feelings were thus excited by the attempt to recall them, and tell them to others.

As many young persons whom I have never seen, and who never will see me, will read the narrative, I must say a word or two to them. You desire to be great. I hope you may be all that your best friends anticipate. But never forget that the first step towards true greatness is to be good. My mother once repeated to me with tones of voice, and an expression of countenance which I never can forget, and I repeat it to you as my most earnest counsel—"*Remember the God of thy fathers, and serve him with a perfect heart and a willing mind. If thou seek him, he will be found of thee, but if thou forsake him, he will cast thee off forever.*"

CHAPTER 1

Situation of Abb's valley

"The Valley," as the expression is understood by those who live in it, denotes the tract of country in Virginia bounded on the east by the Blue Ridge, and on the west by a parallel ridge, called in most of its extent, the North Mountain. It is a fine agricultural district, presenting the advantages which result from a soil generally fertile, hills and vales, numberless springs of pure water that never fail, streams of various sizes that never go dry, luxuriant forests, a climate suited to grains and grasses in great variety, and eminently favourable to health. Its scenery is not surpassed in variety, beauty, or grandeur by many districts in America. From the tops of its mountains, the eye rests on landscapes lovely beyond description.

Here may be seen in one view, the mountain, the hill, the valley, the forest, the meadow, the cliffs, the stream, the farm, the farm-house, the village, the school-house, and the church. A moral, industrious, contented population dwell here; intelligent, yet unostentatious in their habits and manners, and to a great extent the descendants of those who settled in this region when it was a wilderness; and who, while contending with the savage for this fine country, laid the foundation of literary institutions, and formed the churches which have contributed largely to make the population what it is.

Many a dweller in other sections of our happy country turns his thoughts to a region far from his home, and to other days; and exclaims—"The Valley! I love it! It was the home of my youth; and in it are the graves of my fathers!" Peace to their memory. They were a God-fearing and law-abiding people, because they strictly kept the Sabbath holy, and reverenced the sanctuary. Dangers they met with undaunted firmness; hardships and privations with unrepining endurance. The right to worship God according to the dictates of their own conscience, and the advantages of education, they prized above any other blessings which earth could give. To secure the first, they sought a dwelling place in the wilderness, far, far from their fatherland; and for the second, they relied on their own exertions under the blessing of God.

The first settlers in this valley, with few exceptions, were from the north of Ireland. They were the descendants of the Scotch, who, for various reasons, had emigrated to that country, and had taken with them the kirk and the school. They were decided Presbyterians. Deep abhorrence of Popery, and a strong dislike to Episcopacy, were to be expected amongst those whose fathers had felt the oppressions and cruelties of Claver-house; and whose friends had suffered, and fought, and died at Londonderry.

But if they were free from all interference from Popery after they had settled in America, they did not find the same relief from Episcopacy in the valley of Virginia. The Church of England was established by law in the colony, and its ministers, with some bright exceptions, were a very different class of men from those who now officiate in the churches of that denomination in the diocese of the state. If they had possessed the piety which all who know their successors award to them, the history of that church in Virginia, and the moral history of the state, would have been very different tales from what truth compels those to tell who now undertake to write them. Under the management of those men, as soon as Presbyterians formed settlements in portions of territory before unoccupied, parishes were established, and the attempt was made to extend over them the authority of a church to which they felt a settled repugnance. This led to things which were sometimes painful and sometimes ludicrous.

An example of the latter is presented in the following incident, which tradition tells us occurred in what is now, (as at time of first publication), Rockbridge County. A couple were to be married who were both Presbyterians; but the marriage would not be legal unless the rites were celebrated by a minister of the established church. The minister of the parish was applied to, and the parties presented themselves before him. All went on as usual, till the minister, with the bridegroom repeating after him, came to a clause, which has not been retained in the prayer-book as now used in this country, in which the man said to the woman, "and with my body I thee worship." At this the bridegroom ceased repeating, and said, "I'll nae say that; it's idolatry." The minister repeated the clause, and the man firmly refused to respond. All was thrown into confusion, and the couple left the floor.

After a good deal of conference, a sort of compromise was thought to have been arranged, and it was understood that the obnoxious clause would be omitted; but in the progress of the ceremony it was again read, and the man instantly said, with anger flashing in his eyes, "I towld ye I wud'nt say that;" but the clergyman, without seeming to notice what he said, read the next clause, the man repeated it, and thus the matter was gone through with.

As an Episcopal church was built in each county town, the Presbyterians always located their places of worship elsewhere. Hence, there is not in the Valley any village in which a Presbyterian church was built till after the commencement of the revolution. The oldest congregations were in the country; and not a few of the churches now occupied, stand either on the very spot where the first house for worship was built, or they are near it; and in every case the burying-ground was enclosed near the church.

Amongst others, in passing from Staunton to Lexington along the road leading through Brownsburg, about twenty-two miles from Staunton, the traveller will notice a brick church a few hundred yards on his right, and near it a large graveyard, almost filled with the graves of the generations who, for more than a century, have assembled there from Sabbath to Sabbath to worship God. The house that is now occupied, is the third in which the congregation of New Providence have worshipped. The first was a wooden structure, and stood a short distance east of where the road to the church crosses the creek. The second was of stone, and occupied in part the ground that is covered by the present building.

This house was built either in 1745 or 1746. It was an era of no little consequence, and a work of no little difficulty to the people who accomplished it. Some of the traditions of the congregation will illustrate this. At that time there was but one vehicle that moved on wheels in the congregation, and it was a one horse cart. The heavy timbers for the roof and galleries were dragged to the place with one end resting on the axle of the cart, and the other on the ground. The wheels gave way under the weight of the last one, and the people collected and carried it nearly a mile.

It is said that in the year the church was built, the pastor, in visiting through his charge, took dinner on one occasion with a family, by no means amongst the poorest in the congregation. When all were seated at the table, it was seen that there was not both a knife and a fork for

11

each plate. The mother of the family in making an apology, told him that they had saved money to buy a set of knives and forks; but since the church was commenced, they had given it to that object, and must do without them till the next year.

The sand used in plastering the house was carried in sacks on horseback about ten miles; and this was done chiefly by the girls of the congregation. There are those now living who know that their grand-mothers assisted in this. There was then no Committee on Church Extension to aid feeble congregations in building houses of worship, and with the spirit which animated these people, few churches in our country would ask for aid.

The first pastor of this church was John Brown, whose field of labour extended over the principal part of the territory which is now embraced by the counties of Rockbridge and Augusta. The people at that period were not unfrequently disturbed by alarms of Indians; and often the whole of a family would go to church on the Sabbath, because they dared not leave any at home. The father and sons carried their weapons with them, prepared to defend their lives; and a large number of armed men were frequently seen at the church. On one occasion, a musket which had been placed in an insecure position fell, and was discharged by the fall, during the progress of public worship. The first thought was that the gun had been fired by an Indian; and the assembly was at once in a state of perfect confusion, until the matter was explained. Mr. Brown continued his labours as the pastor of that church for more than forty years, and then removed to Kentucky.

Near the upper end of the burying-ground is a marble head-stone, the inscription on which tells that it marks the grave of Rev. Samuel Brown, who died October 13th, 1818. He was the second pastor of that church. Close beside this grave, stands another marble slab, the inscription on which tells that it marks the grave of Mary, wife of Rev. Samuel Brown. The latter, and her father's family, are the subjects in the melancholy legend of Abb's Valley.

CHAPTER 2

Origin of the Name of the Valley

When God formed the covenant with Abraham, he said to him, "*I will be a God to thee and to thy seed after thee.*" In the epistle to the Galatians we are taught, "*that they which are of faith, the same are the children of Abraham,*" and "*are blessed with faithful Abraham.*" In the following pages an instance of God's faithfulness in fulfilling his covenant will be presented; and there is no doubt that many equally plain might be furnished, if the proper steps were taken to collect the facts. The following genealogical sketch is designed to aid in illustrating; the point.

About the year 1726, James Moore and his brother Joseph, left Ireland, and settled in Chester county, Pennsylvania. Joseph died in 1728, whilst engaged in preparing for the ministry. James married Jane Walker, a descendant of the Rutherfords of Scotland. The family Bible which was brought by the Walkers from Ireland, having in it the register for several generations, was in the possession of some of their descendants, since the commencement of the present century. It may still be in existence somewhere in Kentucky; and if so, is either in the possession of someone bearing the name of Walker, or whose ancestors bore that name.

John Walker and his son-in-law, James Moore, left Pennsylvania and settled in Rockbridge County, Virginia, near the Jump Mountain. James Moore died about 1792, and his wife some two years after him. They were both buried in a graveyard near to where they had lived. No stone marks the grave of either, for it was not until a later period that the custom of marking particular graves in that way, was introduced into that part of the country. Their memorial is written on more lasting monuments in the character of their descendants.

Their family consisted of five sons and five daughters. From them have descended Moores in Virginia and Kentucky, quite numerous;

(the oldest grandson was for some time one of the teachers in Transylvania University) Paxtons, Stuarts, McPheeters, Coalters of Virginia and South Carolina, Walkers, Steeles, Harrisons, with many other names in the second generation; and in succeeding generations far too many either to be followed out or enumerated. With the aid of a family sketch prepared in the early part of this century, the writer of this volume has been able to identify many who have descended from James Moore. With gratitude to God he here records, that wherever he has found them, in the third, fourth, and fifth generation, he has found them the servants of God.

The sixth child and second son of James Moore bore the name of his father. He married Martha Poage, whose parents lived about nine miles south of Lexington on the road leading to the Natural Bridge; and after his marriage resided some years at a place on the same road, which was known for many years as Newel's Tavern. From this place he removed to the county of Montgomery, and after a residence of only two or three years there, fixed his house in Abb's Valley, in Tazewell county. This valley gets its name from Absalom Looney, who is supposed to have been the first white man that visited it. It was in about 1766 that the white man first saw this section of the country. A company of hunters is said to have spent several months in the mountains and valleys immediately around where Jeffersonville, the county-seat, now stands.

In the following year some of this party returned, accompanied by several others; and at the end of the hunt, two or three of them, instead of returning as they had designed when they left home, remained with the view of making preparation for the removal of their families, and a permanent location there. Tradition tells that the first corn raised here by the white man, was planted in 1767 or 1768. In two or three years after this, there were several families who had fixed their homes in the various inviting valleys. The names of Bowen, Harman, Carr, Witten, Butler, Peery and Bradshaw, are identified with the traditions of frontier life in this region.

It was in the summer that the first cabins were built here, that the Cherokee and Shawnee Indians had a bloody battle in these mountains. A band of the former tribe had formed a summer encampment near one of the licks which was much frequented by the deer and the elk, to avail themselves of the advantage which it afforded in killing these animals. This party is said to have numbered about two hundred men. A short time after they had encamped there, a larger

14

band of Shawnees came to the same neighbourhood, to occupy the same hunting-ground, and sent a messenger to the Cherokees with an insulting order to leave. He was sent back with a defiance, and both parties prepared for battle.

The Cherokees took their station on the top of a ridge, and constructed a rude breastwork, behind which they awaited the attack of their foes. The battle commenced early in the morning, and lasted until night put an end to it; and was renewed the next day. The Shawnees found that they could not dislodge their enemies, and towards noon drew off and abandoned the effort. A truce followed; both united in burying the dead in one common grave, and then retired to their homes; one to the south, and the other across the Ohio. There were two or three hunters in the immediate vicinity, who witnessed this last conflict of the red men in this favourite hunting-ground.

The valley in which Mr. Moore fixed his residence is about ten miles long, and from one-fourth of a mile to three-fourths wide; and though not deficient in water, there is no stream that runs along it, or across it. The rivulets that come down the mountains, and the springs that rise at their base, sink at the edge of the bottom, and burst out in a large spring near the lower end of the valley. When the white man came here, he found the valley in some parts destitute of any forest growth, and clothed with luxuriant grass; in other portions there were dense thickets of red haw, crab-apple, and the other shrubs which generally are found growing with them. It is a limestone country, and the mountain sides were covered with a magnificent forest growth, under whose shade the wild pea, that most nutritious vine amongst the native herbage of our country, in which cattle delight more than in the rich clover of cultivated fields, and other herbs sprang up in wild luxuriance.

It was a quiet, secluded spot, the very paradise of the hunter and grazier. In the summer, stock required little attention, and in the winter, there were but few occasions for feeding them. The grass which had grown up in the thickets, and which was sheltered from the frost, and the browse on the hill sides, furnished them abundant subsistence. The bear, the deer, and the elk were there in great numbers; besides smaller game in variety and abundance. Everything that an Indian or a hunter would ask for was found there; the hand of industry alone was needed to add the comforts of civilized life, to the rich plenty of native production.

Mr. Moore's attention was turned to this spot by a kinsman of his,

15

who, having visited the south-western part of Virginia to procure ginseng, had traversed this valley and some of the mountains and valleys near it. From his representations, Mr. Moore took an exploring tour, and selected this as the place for his future abode. Many considerations united their influence in leading to this step. The advantages which the place presented were many, and in his estimation very great. It was out of the usual track of the Indians; none of them lived near; stock could be raised with very little trouble; the climate was fine; the soil fertile; game abundant; and ginseng could be obtained in large quantities. Some other families had established themselves in the same region; the attention of many others had been turned thither; and it was probable that in a few years the number of settlers would be much increased.

In making arrangements to take his family there, he went out in the spring accompanied by some labourers, built a cabin, planted a crop, and left an Englishman named Simpson, who had been an indented servant in his family and was then free, but still remained in his employment, to cultivate the crop and enclose more land during the summer. Simpson's situation was lonely in the highest degree. The nearest family was distant from him more than ten miles, with more than one mountain ridge intervening, over which there was not even a path. On one occasion, a man from the Bluestone settlement spent a couple of days with him, and on the third day they agreed to take a hunt; but a thick fog coming on, they both got bewildered in the woods. Late in the evening Simpson found his way into the valley, and reached his cabin after night. The other man spent the night in the woods, and the next day went back to Bluestone.

Sometime after night, Simpson heard what he thought must be the voice of a man calling to him from the other side of the valley. He answered, and the call was repeated. It was extremely dark, and he had no light in the house. Supposing it to be his guest of the previous night, he shouted, "I'll make a light and come to you;" and going into his cabin he lighted some pieces of split pine. Sheltering the blaze from the wind with the skirt of his hunting shirt, he started towards the spot from which the voice had proceeded. When he got pretty close to the edge of the thicket, he threw aside the covering of his light, and holding up his torch called aloud, "Where are you?"

Just as he uttered the words, a wild terrific scream was heard a few yards from the spot where he was standing, and some large animal dashed through the bushes, evidently very much frightened. He then

16

discovered that he had been visited by a panther, and that his torch had saved him from being torn to pieces by it. With no other incident worth notice, the months of his solitary life passed away; and about the middle of autumn Mr. Moore removed his family to the valley. He was accompanied by his brother-in-law, Robert Poage, and Mr. Looney, who has been before mentioned, who each had a small family. These three families fixed their dwellings a mile or two from each other, and for some years no other family resided in Abb's Valley.

CHAPTER 3

Singular Indian Remains

The frontier man and the frontier family of the period to which this narrative refers, are amongst the things of bygone days. Few specimens of them are now to be found. It was necessary that the head of the family should be hardy, fearless, capable of enduring labour and exposure without injury, and able by day or by night to find his way through the forest with the certainty which characterizes the wolf or the Indian. Familiarity with the use of the rifle and the tomahawk, was scarcely considered an accomplishment. It was necessary that every man should possess them. He did not know at what moment all his skill would be called into requisition in defending his cabin against the attack of the Indian. Some knowledge of several different trades was deemed essential in each household. Tools of the carpenter, the blacksmith, the tanner, the shoemaker and the cooper, must be possessed and used.

A young woman who did not know how to spin, dye, weave, and make into garments the cloth that her own hands had produced, stood little chance of finding any man who would ask her to be his helpmeet. Each family formed a sort of independent community, relying on its own exertions to supply its own wants. Owing to their isolated position, the advantages of schools were enjoyed to a very limited extent; but education was not wholly neglected. By the persevering efforts of the parents, all were taught to read and write; the boys were taught arithmetic, and on the Sabbath the Bible and the Catechism were carefully studied in many families. Such a man was James Moore, such a woman was his wife Martha, and such a family was his likely to be in Abb's Valley.

If they formed an isolated community, there is full evidence that a dense population had at one time occupied this valley. Near the place where Mr. Moore built his cabin, there are found clear indications of an Indian village. The stone hatchets, flint arrow-heads, and broken pieces of their rude pottery have been found there in abundance. But beside these, there are found in the country, caves that seem to have been either places for depositing the bodies of the dead, or of depositing their bones after the flesh had decayed. It is said that some of these bones are of an extraordinary size, and some have supposed that they belong to an extinct race that once dwelt in this region. Of the great numbers of skeletons in these caves, some idea may be formed from the following remarks, written in 1849, by a gentleman who had passed through the country:

"There is in Tazewell a cave, discovered not many years since, which contains a large number of human bones. I am sorry that I cannot give the dimensions of the cave, as this would enable us to form some estimate of the number of skeletons it contains. I was not informed of its existence until after I had left its vicinity. This is my only apology for failing to examine in person this gloomy cavern of the dead. When first discovered, the cave's mouth was walled up with stones, on the removal of which the entrance was easy. One who had been in it, told me it was crammed with bones filled up all around. Many of the skulls and other bones were whole at that time. His impression was that there had been tons of bones in it."

If this had been a favourite hunting-ground, or a favourite residence of the Indians, and the sepulchres of their fathers were there, it is not to be wondered that those who first settled there did not find it a safe home. Almost every year, and often more than once in the year, they were alarmed by reports that the savages were approaching. From the threatening danger they took refuge by going to other settlements where there were blockhouse forts, and returned when it was supposed the danger existed no longer. An incident or two gathered from tradition will show the dangers that attended their situation.

Mr. Poage, the nearest neighbour of Captain Moore, was a blacksmith. On one occasion three men had gone from the settlement on Bluestone, to get some work done at his shop; and as he was unable to finish it that day, they had to spend the night at his house. Sometime after dark they all noticed what seemed to be an unusually frequent noise of the screech owl. One of the men remarked rather carelessly, that it did not seem to him to be exactly the noise of the owl, and he would not be surprised if it was made by Indians; but the suggestion did not seem to excite any apprehension, and they all went to bed.

A short time after midnight, the door was burst open. The men sprang to their guns, and one of them, by mistake, got hold of the gun which belonged to another man, and had a double trigger. He placed the muzzle against the breast of an Indian, and in the attempt to discharge it, broke both triggers, and the savage escaped. Finding that there were several men in the house, they made no further attempts to enter it, and after some time went away.

Early the next morning, a young man, whose name was Richards, left Captain Moore's house to place some deer skins in soak preparatory to dressing them. Although he was going only a few hundred yards, he took his rifle with him, remarking that he might see a deer; and if they heard him shoot and call aloud, some of them must come and bring the dogs. A short time after he left, the report of a rifle was heard, and immediately his voice was recognized. Supposing it to be the signal for the dogs, one of the family started with them, and soon found Richards shot through the body, his head gashed with the tomahawk, and the scalp torn off. He died in the course of the day. Mr. Moore immediately mounted a horse, and rode rapidly to Mr. Poage's to warn them of danger, and from them learned what had taken place the preceding night. The three families living near to each other, Moore's, Poage's and Looney's, went to the fort on Bluestone that day. Mr. Poage never took his family back, but sold out to Mr. Moore, and returned to Rockbridge. Mr. Looney remained but a short time longer, and by his removal only one family was left in that part of the valley.

It may seem strange to those who are unacquainted with the fascinations of frontier life, that Capt. Moore did not follow the example of his neighbours; and that in the face of so many real dangers, and after so many warnings of them, he still continued to reside in the valley. It is indeed difficult for those who have spent their lives where they never have thought for a moment that they were in danger, either from wild beasts or savage men, to understand how it was possible that either he or his family could feel at ease for a day. But from his childhood he had been familiar with these dangers, and his wife as well as himself had grown up in the midst of them.

During that part of the year in which they were most liable to be disturbed by the Indians, he always had hired labourers in his family, each of whom was as familiar with the rifle as with his right hand. All had lived from infancy in the midst of dangers, and being accustomed to meet difficulties of every kind, every one possessed a determined self-reliance which could meet without dismay anything that might happen. Familiarity with danger hardens the mind against its terrors. Families live in habitual cheerfulness on the sides of Etna and Vesuvius, although they know that the bowels of these mountains are molten masses, and that at any moment fiery torrents may stream down their sides.

In addition to this, Mr. Moore himself was no ordinary man. We have the best evidence of this from the estimation in which he was held by those who knew him well. At a time when offices in the militia were conferred only on those whom their comrades were willing to trust as their leaders in the hour of danger, he had been selected by those who knew him well to command one of the frontier rifle companies; and as captain, led a company of his fellow mountaineers in General Green's army, in the hard fought battle at Guilford Court House. His was one of the companies that met the first onset of the foe on that memorable day. They were mounted riflemen, and on going into the engagement, had tied their horses in the woods behind the hill, and out of the reach of injury from the balls of the British. After the Virginia militia had performed the part assigned them with much credit, they retreated; and this company sought to regain their horses.

The animal on which Captain Moore was mounted was fleet, young, spirited, and never before had heard the din of battle. To secure it from breaking its bridle, he had passed the reins in a noose over the end of a limb, which allowed the horse considerable room to move about. When he came up to it, he found it impossible to get it to remain still, and leave the reins slack, so that he could unfasten the noose. The rest of the company were all mounted, and the British dragoons were dashing towards them in a brisk charge. One of his men noticing the difficulty, called out, "Cut the reins. Captain; cut the reins!"

"No, I won't," was the instant reply; and springing up, with a powerful jerk he broke the limb. In an instant he was in the saddle, but encumbered with his rifle, and the limb still hanging in the bridle. His frightened horse, instead of following the rest of the company, started directly towards the dragoons. To free his bridle was the work of but a moment; and when within a few yards of the enemy, who felt sure of either capturing or killing him, he wheeled his horse, and its fleetness enabled him to escape. It has been said of him that he never was known to lose his presence of mind in any emergency in which he was placed.

At the close of his term of service, he returned to his home in the valley, the quietness of which must have presented a strong contrast to the bustle of life in the army. He was prospering finely in his business. After having lived eight or nine years in the valley, he had nearly a hundred head of horses, and a large number of cattle, from both of which kinds of stock he made profitable sales every year. Providence seemed to smile on him in everything.

His family were blessed with fine health, and by giving attention to their education as well as he could by his own and his wife's exertions; by the careful observance of the Sabbath, and by attending to family worship, he and his pious wife sought to remedy as far as possible the privations and disadvantages under which they and their children laboured, in being deprived altogether of the privileges of attending on the ordinances of God's house. If the present was almost unmingled prosperity, the future seemed scarce less bright. He had formed his plans, and had almost secured the means to purchase the whole of the valley; and here he designed to settle his children around him, and in the midst of them spend his old age. These were his plans, but the purposes of God were very different. "How unsearchable are his judgments, and his ways past finding out "

CHAPTER 4

One of Captain Moore's Sons Carried Into Captivity

During the interval between the close of the war of the American Revolution, and the treaty made with the Indians after they had been defeated by General Wayne in 1794, the western frontiers were greatly harassed by the savages. The Shawnees, perhaps more frequently than any other tribe, took a part in the inroads on the settlements in Pennsylvania, Kentucky, and Virginia. It seemed to be their plan not to visit the same section of the country very frequently, but to allow time for the settlement to get into a feeling of security after one attack, before they made another. Their feelings towards the whites were bitter. They had been much irritated by some of the occurrences of the war; they saw the settlements steadily extending westward; they had been driven from many hunting-grounds; and many favourite districts which were formerly their dwelling-places, they saw in the possession of strangers.

Their hatred was directed to the race, and not to individuals; and they could scalp and torture with as much pleasure the female and the child, as the intrepid man who had met them in battle. They delighted to come by surprise on a defenceless family, to lead mothers and children into captivity, to gather the spoils of the household, and carry them to their distant *wigwams*. Frequently they did not inflict needless cruelty on their captives. If they encountered men, they sought to kill them; but if women or children were put to death, it was usually in the first attack, and before they were sure of victory.

Sometimes the captives were adopted into a family of the tribe; sometimes they were sold to the French, or to Tories who had removed to Canada; sometimes they were restored to their friends by the terms of a treaty of peace; sometimes their relatives ransomed them; and some instances occurred in which captives became attached to savage life and savage friends, and remained with the Indians of choice, after the opportunity of returning to their relatives was presented to them.

Amongst the Indians who took an active part in harassing the frontiers in the period above referred to, was Black Wolf, an inferior chief of the Shawnees. He lived on the north side of the Ohio, near Chillicothe. He was a man above the ordinary stature, possessing a large share of strength, activity, and courage; and was one of the most stern and vindictive warriors of that tribe. He headed several of the parties that harassed the south-western part of Virginia. Tazewell seems to have been a favourite point of attack; and hence no part of the old frontier was the scene of so many Indian adventures. I have heard at different times, and with more or less particularity, the stories of about twenty of these forays, but must confine my narrative to Abb's Valley, which Black Wolf visited in 1784, when he took captive James, the second son of Captain Moore. James was then in the fourteenth year of his age, already well versed in the use of the rifle, and accustomed to travel over the mountains; an adventurous, keen hunter for his age.

On one occasion when out alone with his dogs, they had fallen on the trail of a large panther, which they had driven to take refuge in a cliff. It placed itself in one of the crevices of the rocks where it could be approached only in front, and there was entirely safe from all attacks of the dogs; and in consequence of a jutting point of one of the rocks, could not be seen except by a near approach. But though the near approach was connected with no little peril, of which he was well aware, James determined not to let the dangerous animal escape. He advanced cautiously with his rifle ready to fire, until at the distance of not more than three yards, he got a sight of it, and instantly shot it through the head.

About the middle of September, in the year above named, he was sent after breakfast to bring a horse from the place where Mr. Poage had lived; the distance was about two miles. He had often gone there alone without fear; but on this occasion he had scarce lost sight of his father's house, when an unaccountable feeling of dread came over him; which became so distressing that he had at one time determined to go back, but was prevented from doing so by the fear of his father's displeasure. He never could explain this fear on any other ground, than that it was a strange presentiment of the evil which was about

24

to befall him. There is, however, one circumstance which I suppose makes the case entirely explicable without the necessity of having recourse to supernatural causes. He had spent the previous night till a late hour, reading the wild tale of Valentine and Orson, in which he was greatly interested; and the influence of the feelings of the past night still existed in his mind to some extent, though he knew not what it was.

The account which he has since given of the matter, and which is here copied from his dictation, is that it was not the dread of Indians, for he was not thinking of them. It was an undefined apprehension of some great calamity that would befall him; that perhaps some wild beast would devour him. In this agitated state of mind he went forward until he had almost reached the field where the horses were, when Black Wolf and two younger Indians sprang from behind a large log, and yelling the terrific war whoop, rushed on him, and laid hold of him before he had time to think what to do. When he first heard their yell, he supposed it was the wild beast which he had dreaded; and was relieved in no small degree when he saw it was Indians. He said aloud—"It is only Indians. I need not be scared. I shall only have to go to the Shawnee towns." Wolf then directed him by signs to catch one of the horses, giving him some salt for this purpose; but as the young Indian retained the bridle, and ran up to James with it when he saw him take hold of the mane of the horse, he contrived to have the horse break away from him. After two or three unsuccessful attempts it was given up. He says he had no wish to have his father lose one of his best horses.

They then started towards the Ohio, the two young men before, James next, and Wolf behind, who with care covered any marks which the others had made. James commenced breaking the tops of the bushes as he went along, but Wolf immediately noticed it, and shaking his *tomahawk* over his head, compelled him to desist. He next began to turn up the leaves with his toes as he walked, but this did not escape the notice of the watchful savage, who at once understood his object in doing it. Coming forward, he showed him how to set his foot flat on the ground, and how to lift it in taking the step without leaving any marks; and with an angry shake of the *tomahawk*, compelled him to obey the directions he had given him. In the afternoon, the rain began to fall, and the evening was quite cool.

About the time that it became dark, the party stopped in a dense laurel thicket, and spent the night without fire, shelter, or food. This

25

was a dismal night to the captive. His clothing was only such as was suited to the hottest part of a summer day; his arms were securely tied with straps of untanned skin; he was placed between the two young Indians, and another strap which Wolf held in his hand was tied round his body. In this situation he revolved in an endless variety of ways all the circumstances of his condition. He had often heard of Indian captivities, of persons escaping from them, and of the cruelties sometimes practised on captives; and anxiously did he endeavour to settle his mind on some probable issue in his case.

Often his thoughts turned to his late happy home; and he vainly wished that he could communicate the knowledge of his situation to those from whom he had been separated so unexpectedly. He well knew that an anxious group would be gathered around his father's fireside that night; and that he would be the subject of conversation, conjecture, and of earnest prayer when the family kneeled together in their evening devotions. Strange as it may seem, he at length fell into a sound sleep, and passed some hours in unconsciousness of the trials that were pressing upon him.

All that his imagination pictured, actually passed in the family that night. In the afternoon, Mr. Moore surprised at his son's delay in returning, went to the field where the horses were, and from various indications, felt convinced that his son had been taken captive, and had not been killed. But Wolf had been so careful not to leave any trace of the direction his party took when leaving the valley, that Captain Moore was not able to find any indications that would enable him to form satisfactory conjectures, either as to the numbers of the party, or the route they had taken. The only point on which he could form a fixed opinion was, that his son had not been killed; but whether he had been taken southward, or toward the Ohio, he could not tell. His son was a captive amongst the savages; but even here hope sought for something to rest upon, and soon found it.

James was healthy, hardy, active, cheerful, and would not be likely to suffer material injury from anything an Indian could endure. And through the traders, intelligence would be gained concerning him, and he would be restored to his parents and to his friends again. Such were the reasonings and the hopes, which in time gave to the family all the alleviation which their circumstances admitted. Often, often, was James the subject of conversation; and various plans were talked over, and some of them executed, to ascertain where he was.

At the dawn of day Wolf and his party resumed their journey, making their way towards the ridge in which is found a low pass that is called Maxwell's Gap. This pass is called by this name, from the circumstance of a man named Maxwell having been killed there in a fight with some Indians. In this gap they halted for a short time, and Wolf brought from the place where he had concealed it on a former expedition, an iron oven, which he required James to carry. At first it was placed on his back somewhat after the manner of a knapsack; but as its weight and position gave him great pain, he threw it down, and by signs expressed his determination not to carry it any further.

Wolf then laid down his load, and bade him take it; but when James found that he could not even place it on his back, he took the oven again, filled it with leaves, and turning it down on his head, carried it without much difficulty or pain. The day after they left the gap, it commenced raining, and one of the young Indians attempted to take James's hat. He understood enough of Indian character to know that all his chance of faring well with them, depended on showing a spirit which would not quail at any appearance of danger, and which would resist everything like oppression. He therefore firmly resisted the attempt to take his hat; and when it was persisted in, he struck his assailant. The Indian then explained that he wanted the hat to protect the lock of his gun from the rain, to which use of it James assented; and when the rain ceased, it was returned to him.

The Indians had no food with them, the chestnuts and acorns were not yet ripe, and they met with neither roots nor berries which they could use as food; and as they pursued the route which could be travelled with the greatest expedition, they kept on the top of the ridges where no game was to be met with. In this condition, they resorted to an expedient for relieving the cravings of hunger which dire necessity had taught the savage. They took the inner bark of the yellow poplar from near the root, boiled it, and drank the decoction with evident benefit. On the third day they killed a bear, but it was so poor the Indians would not eat any of it. On the fourth day they killed a buffalo. As soon as they could, they made some broth from a portion of the intestines hastily washed in the branch that happened to be near, and drank heartily of it.

At night they again made broth, and drank freely, but did not eat any of the meat till the next morning. Had they eaten the meat at first, it would have produced sickness, if not death; but by the course they pursued, no inconvenience was experienced. After this they did not suffer from the want of food; and being now out of danger from pursuit, they travelled less rapidly than at first. After the party felt themselves free from danger, Black Wolf gave one loud, long whoop every evening at sundown, and every morning at sunrise, indicating that he had one prisoner. When within about one day's journey of the Ohio, they stopped for the night on the top of a ridge. A small camp-kettle was given to the captive to go down to the foot of the ridge for water. As he started down the hill, Wolf wrapped himself in his blanket, and lay down as if to sleep.

As soon as James got to the foot of the hill, supposing himself entirely unobserved, he kneeled down and engaged in prayer to God. He had been taught this and other duties of religion by his parents; and now he realized as he never had before the privilege of calling on God, and feeling that though unseen He was a friend near at hand; the only friend to whom he could tell his sorrows; the friend that could guide and protect him. It is said in God's word, *"Thou wilt keep him in perfect peace whose mind is stayed on thee, because he trusteth in thee."* In part at least, this was fulfilled in the case of the young captive. When he had cast himself on God, he rose from his knees in a state of entire tranquillity of mind. So great was the change in his feelings, that for the first time since his captivity the tears burst from his eyes, and he wept abundantly.

From that hour he felt no troublesome apprehension of evil. He had made God his refuge, and God took care of him. When he returned with the water, the marks of the tears were on his cheeks; and Wolf coming up to him pointed to them, and angrily shaking the *tomahawk* over his head, intimated to him that he must cry no more. He afterwards found out that every movement of his had been watched carefully; and that it was a trial of him to see whether he would attempt to escape. From this time he was guarded less strictly.

The party pursued their way leisurely until they reached the Ohio, which they crossed on a raft formed of pieces of dead timber which they found on the bank, and fastened together with grape-vines. They crossed somewhere between the mouths of Guyandotte and Sandy Rivers, and probably near the mouth of the latter. Thence they took the trail to the Indian settlements on the Scioto. During the journey James suffered very much. When he was taken prisoner his clothing was thin, suited to the warm weather of the latter part of summer, and he had on neither shoes nor *moccasins*. But the first night of his captivity the weather changed to the cool temperature of early autumn; and before he reached the end of his journey, he had several large ulcers

"JAMES KNEELED DOWN AND ENGAGED IN PRAYER TO GOD."

on the soles of his feet, occasioned by bruises on stones.

To save his captive from any cruel treatment, Wolf did not take him directly to his own village. But after some days there was a council in the village where he was, at which he was present. An old chief spoke with great earnestness, and by the manner in which he and others looked at him, the captive understood that the speech had reference to him. He learned afterwards that the old chief was reprimanding Wolf for his course in harassing the whites; and warned him and others, that they would draw down on their tribe the vengeance of those whom they were provoking. Not long after this Wolf sold his captive for an old horse.

About this time the season for the fall hunting of the Indians commenced, and James was sent with a party to a distant point, where they were to continue their hunt till after mid-winter; by which time it was supposed the party, beside procuring valuable peltries, would get meat for the latter part of the winter and the spring. Before starting on his expedition, he was left for several days alone in the *wigwam* of his mistress. Some boiled hominy was given him for food each day, but none of the family remained with him. He never learned what the design of this treatment was. During the time of this solitude he often engaged in prayer, and found much comfort in it. Few incidents show the value of early religious instruction more clearly than this does. The good seed had been sown by parental care, and now it bore fruit in circumstances where it was much needed. "*There is a friend that sticketh closer than a brother,*" a friend there is that can help when all other aid is far off; that can console when removed from every other source of comfort. That friend has said—"*I love them that love me, and they that seek me early shall find me.*"

A few days after this period of solitude in the hut, the company started. In this expedition they suffered severely. James fared as the rest of the party. Indeed, he never met with any special ill treatment during the time he was with them. But this year the winter set in early, and the snow fell very deep. They killed very little game, and subsisted almost entirely on parched corn. Their method of preparing it was to parch it, then throw it for a short time into hot water. Each one would take a small handful after it had been a little softened in the water, and placing a single grain at a time on a smooth stone, would strike on it with another until it was crushed as fine as they could well make it; when it was thrown back into the water and boiled for some time. They then drank the water, and ate the corn from the bottom of the pot.

31

This was often their whole living while exposed to the severity of a cold winter in the wilderness, unsheltered by anything except the poor protection of a miserable hut, a thin, small blanket to each, and clothing which would not have been considered more than comfortable in the mild weather of April. To aid them in enduring the hardships which they had to suffer, a large fire was made early in the morning, and each one plunged into the stream usually covered with ice. As quickly as possible they dressed by the fire, then partook of their scanty breakfast, and entered on the business of the day, seldom eating again until they met at the hut in the evening. In this way the captive lad spent the winter, not knowing but that many similar winters were before him. But that God on whom he had called, and on whose care he had cast himself, had better things in store for him.

In the month of April there was an Indian festival at one of the villages near to the one in which James lived, which he attended with the family to which he belonged. Here he met with a French trader, Bateeste (Baptist) Ariome, who saw in him a striking likeness to a son of his who had died a few months before; and on this account, as well as for other reasons, became much interested in him. For fifty dollars paid in goods, he purchased him of the woman to whom he belonged. By Mr. Ariome he was taken to his residence in Canada, not far from Detroit, and was treated as a son. Thus ended his captivity amongst the savages.

After he had been purchased by Mr. Ariome, but before leaving the village, he met with a Mr. Sherlock, a trader from Kentucky, who had once been a prisoner in this same tribe, and had in this way become acquainted with them; and afterwards visited them with goods to barter for skins and furs. Through his agency, a young man named Moffat, whose father lived in the same region from which James came, had been released from captivity. He requested him, on his return, to communicate to Captain Moore the intelligence that he was no longer with the Indians, and had gone to Canada. After several months the message was received, and gave to Mr. Moore the first certain intelligence of the fate of his son; and afforded joy to hearts that had indulged hopes based on they scarce knew what, but still clinging to them, though it seemed as "against hope, believing in hope."

Not knowing how long he would continue amongst the Indians, and in the buoyancy of youth accommodating himself to the circumstances in which he was placed, the young captive had used his best efforts to learn the Shawnee language; and had succeeded to such an

extent that he could speak it with some ease, and understand almost everything that was said in his presence. Amongst other things which he has related as coming under his notice, are some which it may not be amiss to mention.

In the tribe to which his captors belonged, there was a sort of association called the "*Powow* Brothers." No mean, worthless Indian could belong to it, and no female was allowed to be a member. During certain seasons of the year, the brotherhood met frequently, and often remained together for several hours. The object of their meetings he never ascertained. From one of them, the husband of his mistress returned with a serious and even a sad countenance, and sat silent in the *wigwam*.

After some time his wife went to him, and earnestly inquired the cause of his sadness. He told her that during their meeting the Great Spirit had appeared to them; that at first it was not larger than a man's hand; that it increased until it got to be the size of a boy twelve years old; that the Spirit was angry with them and would punish them for forsaking the ways of their fathers. In former times, their paths were marked with the tracks of men and dogs; now only with the tracks of horses. They were more proud, and less kind to one another than formerly, of which he mentioned several evidences. Addressing her, he said in the most solemn manner, "The Great Spirit will punish you for your pride." She was rich according to the Indian notion of riches, and was vain and overbearing.

This took place only a few weeks before James left the tribe; and it is a matter not devoid of interest to know that the prediction was fulfilled. Several months after this, another tribe, provoked by the pilfering of the men of this village, attacked them, and destroyed their town entirely, burning all their *wigwams* and laying waste their fields. This woman barely escaped with her life and her children, losing everything she possessed. James met her in Canada after her reverse of fortune, and gave her a loaf of bread, which she received with the warmest expressions of gratitude.

Whilst a captive he frequently saw large rattlesnakes, but was not allowed to kill any of them. The reason given by the Indians was, that the rattlesnakes were their friends, and therefore they would not allow them to be injured.

CHAPTER 5

Indians Reconnoitring

As soon as Captain Moore was informed of his son's situation, he formed the purpose to go for him and bring him home. But to accomplish this was a thing of no little difficulty. The entire distance was either a wilderness, or inhabited by hostile Indians; and he had no knowledge of the country north of the Ohio. In this state of things, even if he should succeed in making his way to where James was, he could not reasonably expect to be absent from his family less than nine months or a year; and in the meantime he must leave them without a protector. The subject was often talked over, and every scheme that affection and ingenuity could suggest was examined in all its bearings. The result of all was, that for the present the attempt must be postponed. To this conclusion all submitted with the less reluctance, because they knew that James was with a kind man, an intelligent man in business matters, under whose care he would be gaining knowledge that would be useful to him.

In the meantime Mr. Moore was diligently and successfully prosecuting the object which has been mentioned before—the purchase of the entire valley. About a year after the capture of his son, such progress had been made, that the first steps toward securing the title had been taken; and he expected that in another year it would be perfected. But these expectations were destined to meet a melancholy disappointment.

In June 1786, Black Wolf, at the head of between thirty and forty warriors started for the south-western part of Virginia. On the thirteenth of July, they killed a man and his wife, and having plundered and burnt his dwelling, they passed on in the direction of Mr. Moore's residence; and late in the afternoon, reached the foot of the mountain which bounds Abb's Valley on the west. Two of them ascended the mountain late in the evening, and after night approached so near to the house that they were able to count the family when they were at supper. At the usual time all retired to rest, not thinking of any unusual danger. It was noticed that about dark the dogs were much excited, and some horses near the house seemed to be frightened; but this was supposed to be produced by some wild animal, a bear or a panther, that had been prowling about.

Daylight dawned on a happy family in Abb's Valley on the morning of the 14th. They rose early, and engaged in their respective employments. It was the busy, joyous season of harvest. Two men were reaping wheat a few hundred yards from the house. Mr. Moore was giving salt to some young horses not far off. Two of the children had gone for water to the place from which the supply was usually obtained, and which was somewhat in the direction of the spot where their father was. Another had gone to the fence which enclosed the yard to give the signal to Mr. Moore and the reapers to come to breakfast. In this juncture, the fearful war-whoop was heard, and the savages were seen rushing down two ridges of the mountain, one party to the salting blocks, where Mr. Moore was, and the other to the house.

At the first alarm, Mary, who was calling to her father and the reapers, ran into the house, in which were her mother, Margaret, John, and Jane; and Martha Evans, a young woman from Walker's Creek, in what is now Giles County, who happened to be at Mr. Moore's at this time. The house, like almost all the frontier houses of that period, was constructed with a view to defence against the Indians, and was what was called a blockhouse cabin. Amongst other things, the doors were made of plank too thick to be penetrated by a rifle ball, and were furnished with strong fastenings in the inside; and the windows were high and small, and could be secured instantly. In the confusion of the moment, Mrs. Moore and Martha Evans shut the doors and secured the windows, without it once occurring to them that they were shutting out Mr. Moore and the other children.

As soon as he heard the yell of the savages, Mr. Moore started to the house with his utmost speed, and could have got in, if the door had been open; but seeing it closed, he ran past the end of the house, and halted for a moment on the yard fence. This halt was fatal to him, for he was pierced with seven balls. Springing from the fence he ran about forty paces and fell. He was immediately *tomahawked*, and his scalp torn off. Had he succeeded in getting into his house, the opinion of those who well knew him was, that the issue of the attack would have been very different from what it was. There were six or seven rifles in the house, and with the advantages which the construction of the house gave, the defence would have been such as to cost the assailants dear, even if it had not been successful.

The Indians said afterwards that he might have escaped, had it not been for his halt on the fence. Why he made that pause we cannot know. Did he think of some way to rescue his family? Was it only the promptings of an agonized heart without any definite object? We may conjecture about his thoughts in that bitter moment, but we never can know what passed in his mind. William and Rebecca, who had gone for water, were overtaken before they reached the house and killed, and another son Alexander, was killed nearer the house. Simpson, the Englishman spoken of in the former part of this narrative, was in the upper part of the house somewhat indisposed; and Martha Evans, taking two of the guns in her hands, went up where he was, and called to him to fire at the Indians, but found that he was lying on his bed dying. He had been looking out through a crack between two of the logs, and was shot in the side of the head.

When she came down, she raised a plank in the floor, and crept under. Mary was going under with her, but had in her arms the youngest child, an infant, which was crying from the pain of a wound in its shoulder. Martha remonstrated against its being brought under, as it would betray them, and Mary would not leave it. The plank was replaced, concealing only Martha. In this trying moment, when two fierce dogs that had defended the door had been killed, and the Indians were at work with their *tomahawks* cutting it down, Mrs. Moore kneeled with her children, and having commended all to God, rose and removed the bars from the door; and herself and her four children became captives.

There was one son of the family that twice escaped captivity or death. On the day that James was taken, Joseph, his younger brother, was anxious to go with him to bring the horse, but for some reason his parents would not permit him; and thus he escaped at that time. He was not at home on this melancholy day. In the previous spring he had accompanied his father to Lexington, where he had gone to barter the productions of the valley, and procure necessaries for his family. On the way he took the measles, and being too unwell to travel, was left at his grandfather Poage's; and thus made his second escape.

The Indians, having everything now in their power, went leisurely to the work of gathering the spoil. The breakfast which had been prepared for the family, with such additions as were required by the increase of numbers, became the repast of the hungry savages. They were in no fear of any interruption, for several hours at least; for their numbers were such that the few scattered families in the valley thereabout could not muster a force sufficient to attack them with any hope of success. They took out of the house everything they wished to carry away.

Indeed, they first brought out everything, and then made a sort of partition of the spoils amongst themselves, leaving the remainder in a pile to be burned. They then spent some hours in killing all the stock of every kind they could find; and then in the afternoon started for the Ohio, after setting on fire the dwelling house, and all the out-buildings of every description. While they were busily engaged in the division of the spoils on one side of the house, Martha Evans crept from her place of concealment, and unobserved by them, made her way to a ravine not far off, and concealed herself under a shelving rock, on which rested the end of a fallen tree that lay across the ravine. About the time that the party were starting off, one of the Indians passing that way, seated himself on the log, and commenced working with the lock of his gun. He had not noticed her, but she supposing that he had seen her, and was about to kill her, came out and gave herself up, and thus became a fellow captive with the survivors of the family.

Not a few of the readers of this legend will feel more than a little desire to know something of the scenery around Mr. Moore's dwelling, and the state of things existing there when the captives left the valley. I will give them the best help I can in gratifying their wishes, at the same time referring them to the frontispiece for additional aid.

At the distance of about half a mile in front of the dwelling of Mr. Moore, which faced towards the southeast, stood a lofty mountain covered to its top with a dense forest. To the right and left lay the meadow and the cultivated fields of the farm. The house was placed at the foot of a spur which branched off from the mountain that bounded the valley on the northwest. One of the ridges of this spur leads down into the valley near where the house stood, and another a short distance southwest of it. The yard was enclosed by a worm fence, made of rails, and at a short distance from the south-west end of the house there was a deep, narrow ravine. This was the channel of a spring branch, which, opposite the end of the house, poured its clear water over a perpendicular limestone rock, forming a beautiful cascade about ten feet high.

To this place the family usually went for the water that was used for all household purposes, except cooking and drinking. A few paces below the cascade the stream disappeared under another ledge of limestone. A few yards south of the cascade were the blocks where salt was given to the stock; and a little farther in the same direction were the barn, stables, and some other out-buildings. This was the condition of things on the mornings of that fatal day. In the afternoon the scene was sadly changed. Smoking ruins marked the place where the building stood. Sad indeed the day had been to that frontier family; and melancholy beyond description must have been the feelings of that little band of captives as they left the valley with their merciless captors.

When the men that were reaping heard the war-whoop, and saw the Indians rushing down towards the house, they set off as fast as they could run through the wheat field to the woods on the other side of the valley; and as soon as they felt themselves secure from pursuit separated, one of them going to the settlement on Bluestone, and the other going to give warning of danger to some other families. The man who went to the Bluestone settlement was an Irishman, not much accustomed to travel in the forests, and but little acquainted with that region of country. He lost his way, and was some hours longer in reaching the point at which he was aiming than a more expert woodsman would have been.

As soon as provision could be made for the safety of the families there, a small company of men, not exceeding ten, started for Abb's Valley, and reached the scene of the disaster somewhat late in the afternoon; and certainly very soon after the savages had started. Convinced from appearances that the number of Indians was far too great to render it prudent for them to attempt to follow, they hastily buried the bodies of the three children, by placing them together in a sunken place in the earth, and throwing some clay over them, and returned to Bluestone the same evening, to secure the safety of their own families, and raise a larger force to go in pursuit of the Indians.

Joseph Davidson immediately started to Colonel Cloyd, the officer in command of the militia in that part of Virginia. The distance he had to travel was about seventy miles. On the evening of the fourth day, a company of forty men reached the valley. They at once started on the trail with the hope of overtaking the Indians before they reached the Ohio, but afterwards abandoned the enterprise. On their return, they found the body of Captain Moore, and buried it where it had fallen.

The grave was made by removing some earth from the place where a large tree had been uprooted by a storm; the body was wrapped in a saddle-blanket and covered up. A headstone now marks the place, put up many years afterward by his two sons, and the husband of his daughter, bearing this inscription:"Captain James Moore, killed by the Indians 1786."

Amongst the other things taken by the Indians, were three horses, one of which, though very valuable to a man largely engaged in raising this kind of stock, as his owner had been, was so vicious that none of the family ever attempted to manage him, except the Englishman, Simpson, who had been trained to the business of ostler in England. This horse, whose name was Yorick, had never been used for either working or riding, except when Simpson rode him occasionally. Sometime in the second day, the Indians who had hitherto led him, concluded that they would ride him; and one of them mounted him. The horse instantly threw him, and killed him by striking him with his fore-feet. Not daunted by this, another of them attempted to ride him, and soon shared the fate of the first. A third, a large and very strong man, who prided himself on his power and skill in managing a wild horse, then mounted him to subdue him; but with a few plunges the horse threw him off, and laying hold of him with his teeth, killed him also. He was then given up as too vicious to be managed, and was killed. This is the tradition current in that region at this time.

The country between Abb's Valley and the Ohio River is one of the most mountainous tracts in Virginia; and at the period to which this narrative refers, it was an uninterrupted forest. Through this the savages conducted their prisoners with as much speed as they could, encumbered as they were with the spoils gathered in their attack on the frontiers. The fatigues of the journey were met by them and their prisoners with very different feelings. Not feeling secure from pursuit until after they had crossed the Ohio, it was their custom to tie each of the prisoners securely at night, and an Indian lay down to sleep beside each prisoner with the end of the strap in one hand, and the *tomahawk* in the other.

It was understood to be their design to kill the prisoners if any attempt should be made to rescue them. But they did not travel far before they found occasion to gratify their thirst for the blood of their captives. John was a feeble lad, and finding him unable to bear the fatigue of the journey, at the rate they were travelling, he was suffered to fall behind with one of their number, on the second day. When out of sight of the company, his head was split with the *tomahawk*; and the bloody scalp hanging in the belt of him by whom he was murdered, told the mother what had been the fate of her son. The infant was fretful, and was taken from the arms of her mother, her brains dashed out against a tree, and the lifeless body thrown away.

What the feelings of the captive mother were under these accumulated trials cannot be imagined. Truly her cup of sorrow was full; and if anything could make her desire to live, it could only be her two captive daughters. In her circumstances she needed a large measure of the grace of God to sustain her; and although we know not what the exercises of her mind were, there is no reason to doubt that God upheld her; for he hath said, "*I will never leave thee nor forsake thee.*"

The Ohio was crossed at the mouth of Sandy, and then the party directed their course to the Scioto. At several points Black Wolf showed Mrs. Moore the marks he had made on the return from his former expedition, and gave her to understand that it was by him her son had been taken prisoner.

The return of the warriors bringing so many scalps, so many prisoners, and such a rich booty as had been gained in the destruction of the two families in Tazewell, produced much rejoicing in the villages to which they belonged. But in this rejoicing there was one of their number who did not share. The same chief who had reproved Wolf when he returned with James in captivity, again assembled the warriors, and delivered an earnest address to them. The captives afterwards understood that he attempted to convince them, that these plundering expeditions did not weaken the strength of their enemies, and would certainly produce a war with the white man, which would lead to the invasion of their country, and the great injury, if not the ruin, of their tribe. This he clearly foresaw. But the restless, plunder-loving warriors thought not so. They listened to him, but when he had concluded, they shook their heads in token of disapprobation, and went away in sullen silence.

CHAPTER 6

The Captives Disposed of

After Mrs. Moore and her fellow captives reached the Indian towns, they were not treated with cruelty. Martha Evans and Mary were taken to one village, Jane and her mother to another. In being thus thrown together there was some alleviation to their sorrows. The mother and the daughter in one case, and the young woman and the little girl in the other, could see each other every day. The sight of a well-known face would give comfort; and they could talk about the possibility of the success of some plan that might be adopted by their friends to rescue them; and in all the forlornness of their present condition, hope would sometimes cheer them with the prospect of happier days, and paint brighter scenes in the future. With a part of them, these cheerful glimmerings were all illusions. The days of their captivity speedily and unexpectedly came to a tragical end.

A party of Cherokees had made a march to attack some of the settlements in western Pennsylvania, and had been unsuccessful. They were discovered on their approach, were defeated, and some of their number killed. On their return, with spirits chafed by disappointment and burning for vengeance, they came to the towns where the captives taken in the late expedition of the Shawnees were living; and as these were the only white persons in their reach, they determined to put them to death, if by any means they could accomplish it. Their plan was to get the Shawnees drunk, and then they could be induced to join in killing their captives. The first part of the plan was accomplished very easily; but some of the Indian women suspecting their object, removed Martha and Mary, and secreted them at a distance from the town, and kept them there until after the Cherokees had started for their homes.

The precise manner in which Mrs. Moore and her daughter were put to death is not known. It was generally believed that they were tortured with all the cruelty that savage malignity could practise. In confirmation of this opinion, there is the fullest evidence that they were burned; and it is not known that the savages ever burned the bodies of any but those whom they put to death by torture. In this way, this woman of sorrow, whose husband and five children had been murdered in the commencement of her trials, was called to exchange days of exile from her friends, and captivity amongst the savages, for the rest that remaineth for the people of God.

If the last step to that rest was painful as barbarous malignity could make it, in that hour she was sustained by Him, to whom years before she had committed her deathless soul, with all her interests in time and eternity. And who will not hope, yea rather believe, that her daughter, that child of the covenant, the object of the pious mother's anxious prayers in her last moments, passed with her into that blessed abode, *"where the wicked cease from troubling, and the weary are at rest;"* where the good Shepherd leads his flock to the living waters, and the Lord God wipes away all tears from all faces.

A few days subsequent to this bloody scene, the last in the melancholy tragedy of Abb's Valley, Mary and Martha were brought to the town where it had taken place. She missed her mother and her sister. No one told her what had become of them; but when she saw the half-burned bones amongst the ashes and extinguished brands, she knew at once what their end had been. It is not known whether, in the desolation of her heart, she sat down and wept, or whether her sorrow was too deep to vent itself in that way. But this little girl, now in the tenth year of her age, felt that there was still one duty that devolved on her. She got a hoe from an Indian woman, dug as deep as she could in the earth, gathered the bones with her own hands, placed them in the imperfect grave which she had prepared, covered them with the earth, and placed a stone there.

Of her it might be said with truth, "She hath done what she could." Now she was an orphan indeed. She had no parents on earth, but she had a Father in heaven. There is reason to believe that at this early period in her life, her affections rested on him; and that her trust was in him who said, *"Suffer the little children to come unto me, and forbid them not, for of such is the kingdom of heaven."* One fact in her history illustrating the state of her mind may be related in this connection. When the Indians had gathered everything out of her father's house, and had placed in a pile to be burned all they did not design to carry away;

after they had kindled the fire, she stepped to the place, took up two New Testaments, placed them under her arm, and with them started into her captivity.

One of these she retained in every vicissitude, till she was free from all who had injured and oppressed her. Whatever else she may have left or lost, she retained her Testament; and whatever else God may have suffered her to be deprived of, he did not permit his word to be taken from her. When brighter days shone upon her, she could say with the Psalmist, *"Thy statutes have been my songs in the house of my pilgrimage,"*

The Shawnees of the Chillicothe towns had been more successful than most other bands, in their marauding expeditions to the frontier settlements; and the wise and pacific counsels of their old chief had been disregarded; but the day of retribution came. Late in the autumn of 1786, a party of the whites made an incursion into the Indian country for the purpose of destroying these villages. Whether this was a force sent out by the United States, or whether it was a partisan band; where it was from, or who commanded it, are points on which the writer of this story never has learned anything satisfactory. All that he ever has known respecting it was communicated to him by one of the captives. These did not see it. They only saw the work of desolation which had been wrought, and felt its effects. In the first instance, its effects on them were a great increase of their sufferings; but resulted in the speedy termination of their stay with the Indians.

The Indians had but short notice of the approach of their enemies, and the strength of the party that was coming against them. They were convinced, however, that there was no chance for successful resistance; and hastily removing all their effects that they could carry with them, they made their escape into the interminable forests by which they were surrounded. Martha Evans, who, from the movements of the Indians, suspected what was about to take place, endeavoured to give some information respecting herself and her fellow-captive, by writing on the doors of some of the huts, and on the bark of some of the trees with charcoal. It is not known that this was noticed by any of those for whom it was intended.

When the forces reached the towns, they found them entirely deserted, and everything carried off that could be taken away. The scanty stock of provisions for the winter, and the rude huts were all that was left. Fire was applied to these, and everything was consumed. The troops in due time returned to tell of their success; but this expedition, like the plunderings of the Indians, did no good; but on the contrary, produced evil and only evil. Its result was a winter of intense suffering to the Indians, a state of increased exasperation of feeling, and a stern determination to avenge themselves the next summer. If it is right to render evil for evil, then the Indian had as many wrongs to redress as the white man. But if God's law is, *"Render evil for evil to no man;" "if thine enemy hunger, feed him; if he thirst give him drink ;"* then the whole of this system was wrong on both sides; and so much the more wrong on the part of the white man, as he was so much better informed concerning the law of God than the red man was.

When the Indians returned after the troops had left, they saw at once the utter impossibility of spending the winter there. The only resource left them was to go to Canada, and from the French inhabitants, whose allies they had been in the wars that preceded the American revolution, and from the British whom they had aided in that struggle, seek the means of avoiding starvation in the long winter that was before them. No time was to be lost, for winter was at hand, and they had before them a journey of several hundred miles to be made by men, women, and children, through a dreary wilderness in this inhospitable season.

The sufferings of the whole party were very great. At an early stage in their journey the snow commenced falling, they killed very little game, all were scantily clad, their tents were indifferent; and in part of their journey the fruit of the hackberry was almost their only food. This they broke in their iron mortars, then boiled it, and drank the broth. It was in the month of December that they got to Detroit, which was not then as it is now, a flourishing city, with a dense population around it; but merely a military and trading post, with a few scattered inhabitants in its vicinity.

The Indians crossed over into Canada, and spent the winter in the peninsula between Detroit and Lake Erie. In a drunken frolic, Mary was sold for a few gallons of rum to a man named Stogwell, who had been an active Tory during the war, and had removed to Canada after it closed, for fear of losing his life if he remained in the United States.

A little before she ceased to live with the Indians, Martha Evans was purchased from them by a man whose name was Caldwell. He was an unprincipled man, and treated her very badly. How long she remained with him is not now known; but by some means she passed out of his hands, and became an inmate of the family of Mr. Dolson, a wealthy, kind, respectable Englishman, in whose family her situation

"HE OFTEN CALLED HER TO READ TO HIM OUT OF HER
NEW TESTAMENT."

was as comfortable as separation from her home would permit it to be. Thus the young woman and the little girl were both released from their captors before the spring opened, when they set off to return to their place of abode.

Mary's stay with her captors had been attended with peculiar danger. She was placed in the family of an inferior chief, who always showed kindness to her. He often called her to read to him out of her New Testament; and although he did not understand the language, it amused him to hear her read. Sometimes the other children of the family would hide her books to tease her, and pretend that they were lost or destroyed; and one of them was at last lost in this way. When she appealed to him, he always promptly interfered and caused them to be restored. His wife was a woman of violent passions, and sometimes vented them on the children in a storm of rage; but it is not known that she ever manifested any special unkindness to the captive little girl. Her danger came from another source.

It never had been fully settled to which of her captors she belonged, and several of them claimed her. The consequence was, that in the angry discussions of the question of property, they were often on the point of killing her to end the dispute. The young squaws were all kind to her; and it was by their timely interference that she was snatched from danger more than once. Her only means of safety when the subject of dispute had been started, was concealment till the anger produced by it had passed away.

After night, on one occasion, two young women came in haste to where she was, with terror in their countenances, saying, as they drew near, "Run, Mary, run!" She instantly ran from the fire into the forest, so as to be entirely concealed by the darkness, and soon saw the angry disputants come in search of her. It was a very cold night. She had not taken with her the thin blanket which she usually wrapped round her in very cold weather; her clothing was very thin, and to preserve herself from being frozen, she was obliged to move about briskly for several hours before she dared return to the fire. In all these dangers the unseen hand of God was her protection. In his purpose she had some not unimportant service to render to her generation; and till her work was accomplished, her life could not end.

CHAPTER 7

James Moore Hears of His Sister

James Moore had been actively employed, and not unpleasantly situated, in the family of Mr. Ariome. They treated him as a son, gave him good advice, and Mrs. Ariome urged him not to abandon the idea of returning to his friends. He sometimes assisted in the labours of the farm, and at other times accompanied Mr. Ariome in his trading trips. In one of these expeditions, he met with a Shawnee, who had been one of the party that made the attack on his father's family, who told him what had happened to them. This intelligence he received in the latter part of the same summer in which the family was broken up. In the following winter he learned that his sister was in Canada, and heard of her leaving the Indians soon after that event took place.

As soon as he heard where she was, he made preparation to visit her. This was not an easy thing, for the distance was over sixty miles, and the way he must go led principally through a wilderness. To pass through it in the depth of a Canada winter was not only difficult, but attended with danger. Before he could make his arrangements for starting, he met Mr. Stogwell, who informed him that as early as he could travel in the spring, he would remove his family to the neighbourhood in which Mr. Ariome was living; and in consequence of this information, he abandoned the plan of visiting her where she then was. As soon as he heard that Mr. Stogwell had arrived at his new home, he went to see his sister.

The meeting was one of intense interest to both of them. How different was their situation then from what it had been when last they had seen each other in Abb's Valley! Through what toils, and dangers, and trials had both of them passed! What a crowd of recollections would rush into the mind of each! How much would each have to tell the other! But on some accounts the meeting was far more painful to the brother than to the sister. She saw every evidence that his new home was to him a place of comfort, where he was treated with kindness. But everything showed him that her home was a place of deep suffering. Except in point of safety, her situation was worse than when she was with the Indians. He has since told what his impressions were when he first saw her. She was clothed in rags, emaciated and care-worn, the picture of destitution and wretchedness. When far advanced in life, he said he had never seen a person who looked so miserable as she did.

Stogwell, into whose hands she had fallen, was a base, cruel man. He had no feeling of compassion for the orphan girl; and had bought her from the savages, not to do her a kindness, but to make her his slave, and after a few years at most, receive a much larger sum for her ransom than he had paid for her. She never could speak of her treatment in that family, but with deep feeling. In the extremity of her hunger, she often went to the vessel in which the dishes had been washed, and gathered the crumbs of bread that were floating in the water, and ate them. Hardship in every shape was her portion.

Simon Girty is a name that has descended with infamy from the period of the Revolution. There will be occasion to speak of him again in another part of this narrative. But he performed at least one generous act; and as his evil deeds have been handed down, it is but just that the only praiseworthy act which he is known to have done, should not pass unrecorded. He witnessed the sufferings of Mary Moore, and advised her brother to lodge a complaint against Stogwell before Colonel McKee, the British agent for Indian affairs. James acted according to his advice, in the hope that he could get his sister out of Stogwell's possession. In this expectation he was disappointed; but the cruel man was reprimanded, and it was decided that if an opportunity for her return to Virginia should offer, she should be given up without ransom. From this time her oppressor, knowing that his course toward her was watched, was compelled to be less inhuman than he had been.

Martha, James, and Mary were now in the same neighbourhood, and frequently were together. In all their meetings there was one subject of which they never failed to speak, their return to Virginia. But strange as it may seem, there was some difference of feeling about it. Martha had a father and mother, brothers and sisters, and a home to return to. She often thought of that distant home, and all the pleasure she could have there in the society of those she loved. With her, the subject of returning was always one of much anxiety.

With James Moore, the case was very different. His home, his once happy home, was a desolation. His little sister was near him; he had only one brother left, and the family in which he lived had adopted him as one of their own number. There was also in that family a daughter, on whom the affections of his young heart were fixed, and who was believed to return them. It is not a matter of wonder then that he desired to remain where he was, and endeavoured to discourage the other two from thinking of returning to the mountains from which they had been torn, and the scenes associated with all the pleasant recollections of the sweet days of early youth, and the sports of joyous childhood. In his feelings on this subject his sister did not share. Her desires were fixed strongly on the land in which her kindred were dwelling.

While with the Indians there was a feeling of dread constantly present with her, lest she might become reconciled to live with them. She had heard of cases in which captives had become attached to the savages and their mode of life, and had remained with them because they preferred doing so. The very thought that she might do this, filled her mind with horror. She had met with nothing to attach her to anything in Canada; and her thoughts and her affections constantly tended far to the south, to the land in which her father and her mother were born. There, she knew, were many near kindred, amongst whom she would find a home. Martha and Mary were often together; and the young woman and the little girl, whose lots had been cast together in scenes of bitter suffering, often conversed on the subject on which their feelings harmonized so perfectly, and talked over many plans to accomplish that which they so earnestly desired.

They did not know of the self-sacrificing efforts of one who was meeting every danger, and bearing every hardship with unflinching perseverance, whilst endeavouring to find them, and take them to kind friends and kinsmen who had bitterly mourned over their hard fate. God was about to unfold to them the workings of his counsel, and lead them back in a way they had not thought of. We must now go back, and trace the course of another actor in the drama we have been reciting.

CHAPTER 8

Intelligence of the Massacre

Those who are familiar with the frontiers, or the sparsely settled sections of our country, cannot fail to have noticed one custom, which is in a great measure peculiar to them. It seems to have existed from the period of the formation of the first settlements in the country, and is still found prevailing in many regions with all the freshness of a new fashion. The thing to which I allude is, doing much of their work, not by each family labouring alone at its own business, but by neighbours exchanging work and assisting each other. In their heavier operations, such as building their log dwellings and their barns, and rolling together the heavy logs in their clearings, and in other things requiring the strength of many, we can see at once the necessity for collecting more force than is usually found in one family.

But it is by no means confined to operations of this kind. Those who dwell in the solitude of the forest, and cannot see from their own doors the fields or the dwellings of others, and at night cannot hear the barking of any dogs but their own sentinels, are glad of any occasion that brings them to spend a day in the society of their neighbours in the woods. Under the influence of this feeling, though perhaps not conscious what prompts them to do it, to no small extent, the forests are cut down, the fences are put up, the harvests are gathered by what are called in some places "bees," and others "frolics."

To the hard-handed yeomanry, with their simple habits and rural tastes, these gatherings are seasons of no little pleasure. Each expects to do a day of hard work, when he joins a company of his neighbours, either before sunrise or after an early breakfast; and many trials of strength and skill are witnessed, in which intense exertions are put forth for hours together. But they are used to the toil; and the day, and if circumstances admit of it, a part of the night, is spent in not less real pleasure than city *beaux* and *belles* find at their places of public, fashionable resort, or in their brilliant parties. And if the results on health, morals, and happiness are to be regarded, the advantage is greatly on the side of those who, clothed in their substantial homespun, seek their pleasure in that toil which a wise God has appointed to man as the means of procuring his bread.

On the fourteenth of July, 1786, a few men had met on one of the small farms in the settlement on one of the branches of Bluestone, in what is now Giles county, to reap the harvest of John Craw, whose log cabin and other rude buildings marked the recent location of a frontier family. A short time before dinner, when they were resting in the shade for a few minutes, and refreshing themselves with the cool water of a sparkling spring that gushed from the foot of a hill, one of the females of the family was seen coming towards them from the house at a rapid walk. There was something in her manner, which told them, as soon as they saw her, that she was coming on no usual errand. "What is the matter?" said one. "Look how Ann walks."

Their merriment was hushed at once, and one of their number remarked, in a subdued, anxious tone of voice, "Something has happened." Every eye was fixed on her as she drew nearer, and each mind was busy in conjecturing what her tidings would be. When she had approached near enough to be heard, she ended their suspense by saying, "There is dreadful news from Abb's Valley." She then went on to tell them that about breakfast time that morning, as William Clark and Irish John were reaping, they saw the Indians make the attack, and heard the firing of their guns; that they made their escape from the field into the woods; that Clark had started for Davidson's fort, and John for the settlement on Bluestone; that he had missed the way, and instead of passing over the distance in an hour and a half or two hours, he had been five hours in coming; that he found the way at last by finding some horses in the range which he frightened, and they ran home, and he followed their trail.

Long before her story was finished the sickles were gathered up, and they were on their way to the Louse. As soon as possible the settlement was informed of the danger, the families gathered into the fort, and all the men that could be spared, started for the valley. The state of things which they found when they got there, and the course they adopted, have been related in a previous chapter.

One of the company that went to the valley on this occasion was Thomas Evans, a brother of Martha Evans, whose story as connected with Mr. Moore's family has been related with that of her fellow captives. While returning from the scene of desolation, of course the fate of that unfortunate family was the chief topic of conversation. They felt certain that the father of the family had been killed, and as they saw the half-burned bones of a grown person in the ashes of the consumed dwelling, they knew that some one of the family had been killed, and left in the house and burned with it.

It was found out afterwards that this was Simpson, but all was uncertain then; and various opinions were expressed on the subject. In the midst of this talk, Thomas, who took but little part in it, was revolving in his mind the question of going for his sister. It was several days before he hinted to an one the matter on which his thoughts had been employed. When he had formed his determination, he first mentioned the plan to his mother. He did not tell her that he had determined to go for his sister, but in a conversation respecting her, started the inquiry whether it would be possible to rescue her. The question was again and again earnestly discussed in the family, and by them and their neighbours, and viewed in all its bearings before he told anyone that his resolution to go for his sister had been formed on the first day, and that in regard to it, his mind had never wavered.

He well understood from the first all the difficulties of the undertaking, and they were many. It was not known by what tribe she had been taken prisoner. All that was known was, that when leaving the valley, the trail led toward the Ohio, and from this it was inferred that it was one of the tribes living north of that river which had done the mischief; but it could not be ascertained which of them it was, and all the tribes were alike hostile. He dared not, therefore, venture openly and alone amongst them. To do so, would be to expose himself to certain death, or to a captivity scarce less to be dreaded. In these circumstances, how could he begin the enterprise with any prospect of success? How could he learn where his sister was? And if he could gain this intelligence, how was he to gain access to her?

And if he could get to her, how was he to procure her release from her captors, and travel with her hundreds of miles, in the whole extent of which they would be exposed to savage enemies? He thought of all these things, and without being able to see how the difficulties were to be surmounted, his purpose was firmly fixed to commence the undertaking, and under God rely on himself to meet each emergency as it might arise. The man that had the generosity to do this, and the mind which qualified him to succeed in the undertaking, and the cool courage to carry him through all its dangers, deserves to be honoured with a monument more lasting than marble.

After the resolution was announced, it became a matter of much anxiety, and of no little difficulty, to arrange the plan on which the attempt should be made. Thinking it most probable that it was the Shawnees that had carried off his sister, he determined to go to that tribe first. And then it was by no means an easy thing to determine in what manner he should go. His own feelings prompted him to take his trusty rifle, both as the surest means of procuring food, and his best protection in the many dangers to which he well knew he would be exposed. But there were others who thought differently, and it became a point of anxious reflection and of much consultation. The older men, and those best acquainted with Indian habits and feelings, advised that the rifle should be left at home: that he should not appear as a warrior, but as a peaceful man, on an errand of peace, and that he should carry with him as much provisions as would last him till he should reach the Indian towns. This counsel he at length acceded to, and made his preparations accordingly.

It was about the first of September, 1786, that he left his father's, and plunged into the unbroken forests of the west to seek his sister. It was a day of deep interest to the settlement generally, and to his father's family especially. For some time the preparations had been in progress; and on the previous day, an affectionate mother, who had two children at stake in the enterprise, had been busily engaged in preparing the food he was to carry with him. She would not trust that work to any other hands. Many of the neighbours had assembled to see him start; and amongst others, and by no means the least interested of the group, was Ann Crow, to whom he was to have been married in the following month. The whole thing had been thought over, and talked over by them again and again. They could not but feel that they might be parting to meet no more; but on this they did not suffer their minds to dwell.

He felt that he must make the attempt to find and bring back his sister; that if he did not, his future life would be rendered bitter by the reflection, that she had been abandoned to her hard fate without an effort to save her. And whatever may have been the feelings that moved in the lowest depths of Ann's heart, they were repressed, and she was one of those who most steadily cheered him to undertake the enterprise. No one in the company shed a tear, when with his knapsack on his shoulders, his knife and *tomahawk* in his belt, and a trusty pistol concealed under his clothing, he bade all farewell; and, followed by many hearty prayers to God that he would crown his efforts with success, turned his steps toward the Ohio.

Few men could have been found better calculated to succeed in the enterprise in which he had engaged. He was in the full strength of early manhood, healthy, hardy, active, capable of enduring much hardship, an expert woodsman, fearless, cautious, cool, and well acquainted with the habits and notions of the Indians.

Most of the incidents of his travels are now hopelessly lost. The effort to secure them in a form that would not depend on tradition for their preservation, was not made till it was too late. All that is known are the leading points in the story, and some of its details gathered from those who in by-gone days often heard them, but for many years have tnought very little, and talked less about them.

At the period when Mr. Evans started to seek for his sister, the Indians north of the Ohio were constantly committing depredations on the frontiers; but still there were occasional opportunities of access to them. There was always very great risk run by any white man who placed himself in their power; except a few who in time of peace had traded with them. But this risk, Thomas understood fully from the first, was part of the danger he had to encounter. By some means not now remembered, he succeeded in getting into the company of Girty and Conoly, two renegade white men who generally staid amongst the Indians, and were engaged in trading with them. These two men were thought to have instigated much of the plundering which the Indians did on the frontiers. To this day their names and memories are detested, by the descendants of those who were harassed with perpetual uneasiness, from the tampering of these men with the savages.

Evans' feelings revolted at having anything to do with such men; but through them he supposed he might get to one of the Shawnee towns in safety, and then the first great danger would be over. When he met with them, they both professed a willingness to aid him, but at the same time told him that they did not believe that either his sister or any of the Moore family had been taken captive by the Shawnees. He travelled much in the company of these two men; and in the course of the autumn, and winter, and spring, visited twenty-one towns in different tribes, but could not hear any tidings of his sister. He was fully satisfied afterward, that the two renegades had taken active measures to prevent the Indians from giving him the information he sought; and they were aided in this effort by the circumstance which has been mentioned before, that the Indians, amongst whom Martha was, had been compelled to go to Canada.

In the latter part of the spring, he heard that there was to be a meeting somewhere on the border of Kentucky, for the purpose of the ransom of prisoners. To that treaty he went, in company with some of the savages, hoping to meet with his sister there, or at least that he would get some tidings of her. At that place he saw someone who had been a prisoner, from whom he got the information that his sister had been sold to a white man in Canada, and was living not far from Detroit. This at once determined his future course. He went home to get more money, and a supply of clothing, before setting off for Canada.

It was a moment of intense anxiety when he was seen approaching his father's house alone. As each one in succession grasped his hand with eyes filled with tears, no one could gather courage to say, "Where is Martha?" Who can tell the relief that was given to anxious hearts when he, seeing their suspense, said, "Martha is safe with the English in Canada." Then he recounted all the incidents that had occurred from the time he had started. The family had never heard anything of him after he had passed the first fifty miles on his way; and it was a tale of thrilling interest to which they listened. He had been absent rather more than nine months, and these had been months of constant danger and exposure; as almost the whole time had been spent either alone in the wilderness, or in the company of hostile savages. It has been stated already, that most of the incidents of this trip have been lost; but some facts are remembered which show very clearly the great dangers to which he was exposed.

On one occasion he was travelling in company with Girty and Conoly, and two Indians. They halted for a day under the pretext of hunting; and as Thomas had no gun, he was left at the camp. As they had stayed away much longer than he had expected, he determined to leave the camp and go on, and leave them to overtake him that evening. He accordingly arranged everything, and having fastened a stick in the ground, he made a slit in the top, and placed a leaf in it, to point out to them the direction he had taken.

Just as he was about starting, he saw the four coming toward the camp with their faces painted black. This at once told him that an attempt would be made to take his life. If he had been fully armed, it would have seemed a hopeless thing for him to contend with the four; how much more desperate was his condition, unarmed as he was! Retaining his presence of mind, and keeping his eye on every movement, at the distance of about fifty steps, he saw two of them level their guns to shoot at him.

At this instant he sprang behind a small sugar maple, not more than half the thickness of his body, which, of course, left him much exposed. Both rifles were fired, and he felt himself untouched. He immediately sprang to another small tree, and the other two discharged their rifles at him, but missed him. As all the guns were then empty, he started to run, and the four pursued. After he had gone a short distance, he noticed a tall tree lying across his course, which, resting on some of the limbs and the roots, was raised so much from the ground as to render it doubtful whether he could spring over it, and certain that he could not pass under it without a fatal loss of time. Neither could he pass round either end of it, without such a loss of distance as might enable one or more of them to overtake him; for, casting a look behind, he discovered that they had noticed the state of things sooner than he had, and that one of them was bearing to the right, and another to the left, with the view of intercepting him.

As he came near the log, they all shouted; but gathering his strength for an effort on which his life depended, he succeeded in leaping over. Three of the pursuers gave up the chase, and the other only followed to assure him that if he would come back they would not hurt him. When he came back he found three of them washing the black off their faces, and the fourth engaged in plundering his knapsack. Taking hold of one of the guns that was lying near, he levelled it at the man, and told him he would shoot him if he did not return everything he had taken out. The man thus threatened, looked to his comrades, but finding that they showed no disposition to interfere, he was compelled to give up all. Thomas asked no explanation of the cause which had led to the attempt to kill him, and they never said anything to him about it.

On examining, he found that both of the bullets which were first fired at him, had cut the bark of the tree behind which he was, and this had so changed their course that they had missed him. After this he travelled in the company of Girty and Conoly, at different times, more than two hundred miles, and on other occasions he was shot at with the rifle seven times; both the sleeves of his coat were cut with the bullets, but he never was wounded. The circumstances attending any of these attempts to kill him are not now remembered. He never felt himself safe, and said that he never slept so sound that he did not hear every movement that was made.

Before Thomas could get his preparations made for starting to Canada, the season was so far advanced as to render it certain that he could not reach Detroit before winter, and he was compelled to put off commencing his journey till the spring was somewhat advanced. When he set off he did not know how long it would take him to pass through the wilderness to the settlements in Canada, where his sister was; but from his past experience he was fully aware that perils attended him at every step. I have not been able to learn any of the incidents of this tour, previous to the time when he reached Canada, except one.

It was judged best that this journey should be made on horseback. On the route which he determined to take, which led down New River, there lived a man whose name was Hays, that bore the reputation of being a horse-thief. Mr. Evans did not know exactly where this man resided, though he had an impression that after having passed a given locality, he would be out of danger from him. Late in the evening of the day during which he had supposed he was on the dangerous ground, and after he thought he had passed Hays's dwelling ten miles or more, he came to a pretty, good-looking cabin, and asked the man of the house whom he found sitting at the door, whether he could stay there all night, and what he would take to insure the safekeeping of his horse till morning. The reply was, "You can stay, and I will insure the safety of your horse for a dollar."

Evans agreed to give this. After his horse had been disposed of, and he had been in the house some time, his host inquired what had made him so anxious about his horse, and willing to give such an extravagant price for its safe keeping. Thomas replied by telling him on what errand he had started, and the importance of his horse to him in the journey that was before him, and that he had been told that there was a man named Hays who lived on that road somewhere, who bore the reputation of being a horse-thief; that he supposed he had passed his house about ten miles, but that he did not yet feel entirely safe. To his great surprise the answer was, "My name is Hays, and there is no other man of the name living in this part of the country. My enemies tell lies upon me, and I do not blame you for your caution." The horse was safe the next morning. Hays refused the dollar, and on parting expressed the warmest interest and most earnest wishes for the success of Thomas in the long and dangerous journey he had before him.

It was late in the month of August, when Thomas rode to the gate of a yard which enclosed a house that indicated wealth and taste in its possessor. Betsy Dolson was standing in her father's door, when she observed a stranger dismount from a jaded horse, and take the path that led to the house. He was then at the distance of about one hundred yards. After looking at him for a few moments, she said to a young woman, who was engaged in a part of the room from which she could not see the path, "Martha, that is your brother who is coming up the path."

"O no," replied Martha, "my brother is many hundred miles off."

When he had come within about twenty-five steps of the door, Betsy turned away from it, and said, "That is your brother, for he walks like you, and looks like you."

Soon the brother and sister were locked in each other's arms. She only said, "Are they all alive?" and heard him say "Yes," when the feelings that had been pent up for more than two years, found vent in a gush of tears. My reader may imagine what were the feelings of that brother and sister, but I will not attempt to describe them. Many subjects of deep interest were talked over by them before they laid their heads on their pillows that night, for each had much to communicate. He had the tale of his adventures in his efforts to find her, and something of family matters, and more of neighbourhood affairs to tell; and she had the history of her captivity, with all its incidents.

For the first time he learned what had become of the members of that family in whose fate his sister had been so involved, and was not a little surprised when he found that James and Mary Moore were in the neighbourhood in which he had found his sister. Sweet were the slumbers of Thomas that night, and the dreams of Martha were about her distant home, to which she now hoped to be restored speedily.

CHAPTER 9

Arrangements for Their Return to Virginia

Thomas Evans had now accomplished part of what he had under-taken. He had found his sister, but the hazard and difficulty of taking her home were yet to be encountered. As soon as he saw Mary Moore, she expressed an earnest desire to go with them, and although restor-ing her to her friends had not formed a part of his plan, his generous heart disdained the thought of leaving her in her cruel bondage. James Moore was rather more than willing to remain where he was. He was now in his seventeenth year, an active, hardy young man; and when the question was presented to him whether he would let his sister set off for Virginia under the protection of Mr. Evans alone, he felt that it would be base in him not to go with her. He would have preferred that she should remain where she was, and after a year or two come and live with him in the home which he thought he would, by that time, be able to offer her. But when he saw that her whole soul was centred on the prospect of returning to her kindred, he concluded to be one of the party, and, after seeing his relations, to return to Canada.

To get all things prepared for this journey was not the work of a day. It was about the middle of October that the preparations were completed, and the four set out, not knowing what things might befall them by the way. A company of traders that were starting on a trip amongst the Indians, and who were going in boats to the opposite side of Lake Erie, took two of them, and the luggage of all, to the Moravian towns, where they were joined by the other two who had travelled round the end of the lake with the three horses they had for the trip. And here the providence of God found protectors for them through a dangerous part of their journey.

The Indians of these towns had been instructed by the Moravian missionaries; many of them were pious, all of them opposed to war, and desirous to pursue their own avocations, and live peaceably with all men. The massacre of the inhabitants of these villages, at a time subsequent to the period of this narrative, forms one of the dark chapters in the bloody annals of man's cruelty and wickedness. It also shows the influence of the principles of Christianity, in the manner in which these deeply injured sons of the forest, who had been brought under its influence, met their fate at the hands of their bloodthirsty murderers.

A party of these Indians was almost ready to start on their fall hunt, and the route which they designed to take was that which Thomas Evans and his party were to travel. They were anxious to travel with them for two reasons. A few days before they started from Canada, they learned that a son of Simon Girty had formed a plan to waylay them in the wilderness, kill Thomas and James, and bring the two girls back to captivity, and had hired some Indians to aid him in his villainy. But while he was waiting for them to start, he had a violent quarrel with his father, and was so much exasperated at the result, that he committed suicide. And though he was dead, they did not know but that some other person, equally vile, might attempt to execute his plan, against which the presence of these Moravian Indians would be an effectual protection.

And moreover, the route to the hunting-grounds would cross tracts of country frequented by some of the most hostile of the Indians, who would be much less likely to disturb Thomas and his company, if found with other Indians, than if found alone. They, therefore, waited a few days for them, and afterwards found they had acted wisely. One evening their encampment for the night was quite near a party of Indian hunters, and the next morning five of the warriors came to them painted as if for war. They had a long conference with the Moravians, and at last went away without doing any violence; for which result this defenceless party were indebted to the friendship of those in whose company they were.

After leaving them, they had about five days' travel before they would reach the first settlements in Pennsylvania; and during four of these days they knew they were beset with perils. On the forenoon of the last day but one before they got out of the wilderness, they came to the place where a party of savages had encamped the night before, and had left the spot so late in the morning that their fire was still burning. This excited their apprehension of danger very much. They travelled that day, keeping a careful look out, and lay down at night not without fear that they would be disturbed before morning.

Thomas had given them particular instructions about the streams and other landmarks that would guide them in case anything should separate them from him, and a plan for acting in case of an attack by day or by night was arranged. Thomas would bear the brunt; and the others were to escape, and be careful to keep together; and whatever might befall him, they could reach the settlements in the neighbourhood of Fort Pitt. On the night of this anxious day, they put out their fire soon after dark, and lay down, wrapped in their blankets. Before any one of the party had fallen asleep, they heard something stepping along the track on which they had travelled. It sounded to them exactly like the footsteps of a man walking carefully in the dark. A hasty whisper passed around the anxious group.

Nearer and nearer the step approached, and then suddenly stopped. Just as they were on the point of springing up, the snort of a deer was heard, and the innocent cause of their alarm bounded off amongst the bushes. The next day passed without any occurrence to excite their apprehensions, and at its close they felt themselves out of danger, as before the evening of the following day they would be within the frontier settlements of Pennsylvania. When they had arranged everything for the night, the conversation became more animated than on any evening since they had started from Canada. They talked cheerfully of past dangers, and even ventured to chat about the bright future that was now before them. In after days, speaking of that evening, Thomas used to tell, that as they were in the midst of their cheerful conversation, Mary remarked: "Well, Thomas, I never can forget your kindness to me."

Without noticing her countenance as she spoke, he replied; "Oh, when you get home you will be amongst your rich kindred, and will soon forget me."

As he finished the sentence he looked at her, and to his surprise saw her eyes filled with tears, as she said with deep earnestness, "No, Thomas, whatever my future lot may be, I never can forget you; and if ever I have a house of my own, the time never can come when the door will not be open to you."

Many years after both Thomas and Mary were dead, his son, in relating this little incident to her son, said that the last time he ever heard his father mention it, he followed it with the remark, "There is no person on earth I would be so much rejoiced to see as Mary Moore."

It was near the middle of November when the little party arrived at the residence of some of the relatives of Thomas and Martha. Amongst them Thomas designed to remain a short time to rest, and prepare for the remaining part of their journey. The hand of the Lord had been upon them for good, and he had delivered them from those that lay in wait by the way. The danger was now past, and henceforth their journey would not be in pathless forests amongst enemies, but in the midst of those who, from sympathy in their sufferings, would extend to them all needed aid in the several hundred miles that must yet be passed over, before Martha would see her home, and James and Mary would be amongst their kindred. The plan was to remain but a short time, and cross the Allegheny mountains before the winter set in.

But in a few days after they had arrived at their place of temporary rest, Thomas dislocated his shoulder, and in an unskilful attempt to set it, his arm was broken above the elbow; and long before he was able to travel winter was upon them. At that time the settlements were so sparse on the route from Fort Pitt (now Pittsburgh) to Winchester, and the road so little travelled, that it was deemed unsafe to attempt the journey with the girls in company before spring; and when the route was deemed safe in the spring, for some cause not now known, it was thought best that Martha should remain where she was, while Thomas should go on with James and Mary, and return for his sister. They followed Braddock's military road to Winchester; thence took the route usually travelled up the valley to Augusta, where the Moores found the first of their kindred.

But two incidents in this last part of their journey were ever mentioned by them. While waiting for breakfast one morning, Mary took out the Testament which she had carried through all the dangers and sufferings of her captivity, and spent the time in reading it. When summoned to breakfast she laid it down, and when she started forgot it. It was not known that she had left it, until after they had passed over several miles, and she then proposed to return for it, but there was not time to do this, and get to the only house where they could spend the night. To lose it thus, was no small trial to her. It was the only thing she had taken with her from the ruins of her home, and it had been her instructor and comforter in the dark days of sorrow and suffering.

Doubtless the God who had protected and guided her in her whole course, had some end to accomplish by this.

The book may have been left in a family where there was no part of the word of God, while she was going where she would have opportunity to read the sacred Scriptures. It may have been used to instruct others who were without an instructor, as it had instructed her when removed far from all opportunity of attending on the ordinances of God's house. After the lapse of more than sixty years, there is no probability that it has not long since been worn out and destroyed; but if it has been preserved, and could now be identified, what an interesting relic would it be to the descendants of her who prized it so highly!

The last day of their journey was a day not to be forgotten by them. On the morning of that day Thomas paid out the last shilling he had. This occasioned him no uneasiness, as he knew that a few miles would take them to those who had heard the sad tale of the breaking up of Captain Moore's family, and from any of these he felt sure that he and his party would receive a hearty welcome. The day was one of alternate snow and rain. When they approached a farm, which Thomas had found by his inquiries was occupied by a family that had known the story of the misfortunes of those who were under his care, he cheered them by telling them of the kind reception they would meet, and that as it was such unfavourable weather, they would spend the rest of the day and the night there.

But when they presented themselves, their clothes wet through and their limbs chilled with the cold, the reception they met was more chilling than the storm without. No invitation was given them to remain, no interest was manifested at seeing the captive children brought back. Thomas was indignant at this conduct, and, therefore, scorned to ask as a favour that which he thought they should consider a privilege to give. After remaining a short time they started out into the storm, and after this disappointment they would not run the risk of such another reception. They knew that before bedtime they could get to a place where they would be received very differently.

The storm they did not fear. They had often encountered far worse when they had no such hope as that which now cheered them. Sometime after dark they got to the residence of William McPheeters, about eight miles from Staunton. Mrs. McPheeters was the sister of Captain Moore, and here James and Mary met their grandfather and grandmother. The arrival of the guests of that night was unexpected to the family. But here Thomas began to receive his reward for the generous kindness he had shown to the orphans. That reward was in the melting of hearts which he witnessed in the meeting of that evening.

The aged grandparents were deeply affected, and every heart sympathized with them. "There were tears, and there were smiles, there was joy and there was sorrow." Those who had wept over the destruction of the family, rejoiced and wept to see the remnant brought back. This night ended the wanderings of James and Mary; not quite three years after Mary's had commenced, and five months short of six years after James had been taken prisoner.

After resting a day or two, Thomas went on to Rockbridge county, and received from the administrator of Captain Moore's estate, the full amount of all he had expended ir defraying the expenses of James and Mary on their journey, but entirely refused any additional compensation. Sometime in the summer he returned for his sister, whom, as has been stated, he left in Pennsylvania. Then the object to which he had devoted himself for nearly three years, and in which he had endured so many hardships, and had been exposed to so many dangers, was accomplished. He saw his sister the happy member of a family made happy by her return.

How great his pleasure must have been! Generous, noble young man! You have had your reward in part. All that you asked, was the happiness of seeing your beloved sister under the paternal roof again, and this you did see. But the orphan's God gave you more than this; and in the cherished recollections of those who trace their lineage to the captives of Abb's Valley, your name lives, and will live, honoured and revered, for your self-sacrificing devotion to the welfare of others. And the thousands who may read this narrative, will remember your unostentatious heroism with admiration.

CHAPTER 10

Subsequent History of the Captives

Nothing of romantic character remains in the history of those who went into captivity from Abb's Valley. And yet there is no doubt that each reader who has followed them to their return, would feel disappointed if the narrative should be closed there. "What became of them? I should like to know something of their future history," would be the question and the feeling of every mind. As far as the materials for answering the question are at hand, they will be used.

Thomas Evans and Ann Crow were married in the autumn after his sister arrived at home. The next spring he removed to Kentucky, and lived in Shelby county, until sometime in the year 1809. He then removed to Indiana, and settled in what is now Washington County, and near to where Salem, the county seat, now stands. It was then the frontier, and was often exposed to danger from the savages. More than once when past the prime of life, he was a volunteer in detachments of troops that were sent against the Indians, and sometimes was one of the spies that were sent out to watch their movements when danger was apprehended.

In these expeditions his knowledge of Indian habits was much relied on; and though an old man, he was considered a desirable companion in these seasons of danger. He became the father of six sons and six daughters, some of whom reside now (1854) on and near the farm owned by their father. He was a member of the Presbyterian Church, and died in September, 1829.

Martha Evans married Mr. Hummer. Two of her sons, William and Michael, entered the ministry in the Presbyterian Church. She spent the last years of her life in Salem, and was a member of the Presbyterian Church there. She lived beloved and respected by all who knew her. Her death happened in the winter of 1827.

James Moore expressed a desire and design to return to Canada, for some time after he had been amongst his friends in Virginia, but at last abandoned the plan. Early in life he married a Miss Taylor, of Rockbridge County, settled on the farm which his father had occupied in Abb's Valley, and became the father of a numerous family, who, with few exceptions, reside in the same section of country. At an early period after he had gone to reside in the valley, he became a member of the Methodist Church, and continued in the communion of that church until his death, which occurred in the autumn of 1851. He was spared to see his descendants of the third generation.

Joseph Moore, who twice narrowly escaped captivity, lived in the same neighbourhood, a pious man, blessed with a pious family, and died in the winter of 1848. He was an active, useful member of the Methodist Church.

Mary Moore lived with her maternal grandmother for two or three years after her return to Rockbridge, and afterward had her home in the family of Joseph Walker, who was married to her father's sister. His family belonged to the Fuelling Spring congregation, the pastor of which, at that time was the Rev. Samuel Houston. In a letter written in 1836, he says:

> When I first became acquainted with your mother, she was a mild, sweet little girl, living in her uncle's family. When I conversed with her on the subject of religion, she gave evidence of having obtained a saving knowledge of the truth. In consequence of this, I advised her to be baptized, and become a member of the church in full communion. Not long after, when her uncle presented a child for baptism, she, of her own accord, stepped up beside her aunt, and thus by her own act was consecrated to God, and shortly after was admitted to the Lord's table. She continued to reside in her uncle's family more as a daughter than as a niece, was very affectionate to all, and her affection was reciprocated by young and old. Her worth will never be forgotten by those who knew her.

In October 1798, Mary Moore was married to the Rev. Samuel Brown, pastor of New Providence church. In the active discharge of the duties of this station, she passed many happy, busy years. There are two records of her worth. One of these is in the memories of those who were her neighbours, and the people of her husband's pastoral charge. With them her memory is fondly cherished. Few of those who were her equals in age now remain. Like her, they have finished their work on earth. But while those survive who grew up after her removal to that congregation, and while their children continue to worship in the church in which her husband preached, those who look on the marble that marks her grave, will remember her with tenderness and respect. She lived the respected wife of a beloved pastor; a man who was regarded by those who best knew him, as the equal of the most distinguished ministers of his day, in the Synod of Virginia. And no one ever thought that he was wedded to one who was his inferior. In her sphere, she lived as much respected as he did in his.

The other record of her worth is the family that she brought up. She was the mother of eleven children. Of these one son died in infancy, and one daughter in early youth. Seven sons and two daughters lived to mature life.

In no part of her life did her character shine more brightly, than when she was left a widow with this family of ten children, the youngest of whom was less than two years old. This event occurred on the 13th of October, 1818. The precious Sabbath was a communion Sabbath in the New Providence church. During all the services of this sacramental meeting, Mr. Brown seemed more than usually animated, and preached with more freedom and power than common. It is a singular coincidence that on Saturday his forenoon discourse was a lecture on the last chapter of the book of Revelation, which was the last of a course of lectures that had commenced with Genesis. From various causes he had been prevented for several Sabbaths from delivering this lecture.

His oldest son who heard it, has a distinct recollection of the freedom, and solemnity, and power of that discourse, and of the deep feeling which he manifested when speaking of the solemn account which he must render at God's bar for what he had spoken in explaining and enforcing the truths of the Bible, and his solemn appeal to the Searcher of hearts, that he had honestly endeavoured to declare the whole counsel of God. In administering the Lord's supper on Sabbath, he was so carried away by his feelings in his address to the communicants at the last table, that he forgot to distribute the cup, and was about to close the service when one of the elders reminded him of the omission.

On Sabbath afternoon, and on Monday, he delivered two discourses which were regarded as sermons of unusual ability, and were for a long time spoken of by the congregation, as amongst the most striking they had ever heard from him. On Tuesday he ate a hearty dinner, and soon after engaged in some active exercise. This brought on an attack of pain in the heart, and in less than half an hour he ceased to breathe.

In the *Evangelical Magazine* for December, 1818, in an article headed, "An Excursion to the Country," written by the late John H. Rice, D.D., an intimate friend of Mr. Brown, is found a notice of this sad event.

The record of this day (14th of October), presents something like a map of human life. In the morning we were gay and cheerful, amusing ourselves with remarks on the comparative genius and habits of our countrymen, and a thousand things just as the thoughts of them occurred, anticipating a joyful meeting in the evening with some well tried, faithful and beloved friends; when suddenly, as the flash of lightning breaks from the cloud, we were informed of the death of one of the choicest of those friends, and one of the most valuable of men, the Rev. Samuel Brown.

The road which we should travel led by the house in which he was accustomed to preach, and on inquiring for it, we were asked if we were going to the funeral! Thus in a moment was hope turned into deep despondency, and gladness of heart exchanged for the bitterness of sorrow. We journeyed on in mournful silence, interrupted by occasional remarks, which showed our unwillingness to believe the truth of what had been announced, and how reluctantly hope takes her flight from the human bosom. It might have been a fainting fit, an apoplectic stroke mistaken for the invasion of death, and still he might be alive. The roads trampled by multitudes of horses, all directed to the dwelling of our friend, dissipated the illusion, and convinced us of the sad reality.

Still, however, when we arrived at the church, and saw the people assembling, and the pile of red clay (the sure indication of a newly opened grave) in the churchyard, it seemed that we were for the first time assured that Samuel Brown was dead. Only a few of the people had come together on our arrival. Some in small groups were conversing in a low tone of voice, interrupted by frequent and bitter sighs, and showing in strong terms how deeply they felt their loss. Others, whose emotions

71

were too powerful for conversation, stood apart, and leaning on the tombstones, looked like pictures of woe.

Presently the sound of the multitude was heard. They came on in great crowds. The elders of the church assisted in committing the body to the grave, after which a solemn silence, interrupted only by smothered sobs, ensued for several minutes. The widow, surrounded by her children, stood at the head of the grave, exhibiting signs of unutterable anguish, yet seeming to say, "It is the Lord, let him do as seemeth him good." After a little while, on a signal being given, some young men began to fill the grave. The first clods that fell on the coffin gave forth the most mournful sound that I ever heard.

At that moment the chorister of the congregation was asked to sing a specified hymn, to a tune which was known to be a favourite of the deceased minister. His voice faltered so that it required several efforts to raise the tune; the whole congregation attempted to join him, but at first the sound was rather a scream of anguish than music. As they advanced, however, the precious truths expressed in the words of the hymn seemed to enter their souls. Their voices became more firm, and while their eyes streamed with tears, their countenances were radiant with Christian hope, and the singing of the last *stanza* was like a shout of triumph.

The words of the hymn are well known to many, but we think it not amiss to record them here.

When I can read my title clear,
To mansions in the skies,
I bid farewell to every fear,
And wipe my weeping eyes.

Should earth against my soul engage,
And hellish darts be hurled;
Then I can smile at Satan's rage,
And face a frowning world.

Let cares like a wild deluge come.
And storms of sorrow fall;
May I but safely reach my home,
My God, my heaven, my all.

There shall I bathe my weary soul
In seas of heavenly rest.

And not a wave of trouble roll
Across my peaceful breast.

By the time these words were finished, the grave was closed, and the congregation in solemn silence retired to their homes. We lodged that night with one of the members of the church. The family seemed bereaved as though the head of the house had just been buried. Every allusion to the event brought forth a flood of tears. I could not help exclaiming, 'Behold, how they loved him!' And I thought the lamentation of fathers and mothers, of young men and maidens over their departed pastor, a more eloquent and affecting eulogium than oratory with all its pomp and pretensions could pronounce. After this I shall not attempt a panegyric. Let those who wish to know the character of Samuel Brown, go and see the sod that covers his body, wet with the tears of his congregation.

The death of the father of the family devolved on the mother a heavy additional amount of care and responsibility, but she met it in the strength of God, and was sustained. A day or two after the sad event, she remarked to an intimate friend who had come to sympathize with her, "When I look over my past life, and remember through what God has brought me, I do feel that it would be unspeakably sinful in me to indulge for one moment any fear that he will not take care of me and mine. I do cast myself and my children on his promises. I do not doubt their fulfilment, and in this I have strength and comfort."

With these views she met her increased responsibilities, not bowed down in despondency, but with a spirit of unrepining submission, and girded herself to the task laid upon her, strong in the Lord and in the power of his might. In her case was seen the fulfilment of the passage in God's word, which was the text from which her husband had preached his last sermon:

Even the youths shall faint and be weary, and the young men shall utterly fall. But they that wait on the Lord shall renew their strength; they shall mount up with wings as eagles; they shall run and not be weary; they shall walk and not faint.

The religious instruction of the children and servants she had considered her special field of duty before her partner's death. To this she attended with exemplary fidelity. On the evening of the Sabbath, both the children and the servants were carefully instructed in the Shorter

Catechism; and on that day the servants were taught to read. The result was, that almost all of them learned to read with facility in the Bible, and committed the Catechism to memory. After her death, the seed which she had sown sprang up, and four out of six of the grown servants made a profession of religion. Her example was to her family a steady light, holding forth the word of truth.

Of her it may be said with perfect truth, she was "diligent in business, fervent in spirit, serving the Lord." There was no other thing in regard to which she was more careful, than the strict sanctification of the Sabbath-day. When from any cause the members of the family generally were prevented from attending church, every proper expedient was resorted to, to fill up the day profitably, and prevent it from becoming a weariness to those of her household who were not pious. In varied instruction the day passed away, not unpleasantly to any, and profitably to all.

The tenderness of her feelings, her acquaintance with the truths of the Bible, her fervent and deep-toned piety, made her excel in prayer. Before the death of her husband, when he was from home, she led the devotions of the family, and none who heard her will ever forget the impressions produced under her prayers. Out of the abundance of the heart words came with fluency, and in a peculiar manner she seemed to realize the presence of her covenant God. In humility, and in that earnestness which could not be contented with a denial, she pled with the God whom she loved with a pure heart fervently. She lived to see her heavenly Father graciously answering the prayers which she offered for the conversion of her children.

The oldest child of the family was received into the communion of the church, the spring following his father's death, and not long after the next two, and soon after the next two. Each of the children made a profession of religion early in life. The oldest was further advanced when this step was taken, than any of the others, and he was less than twenty years of age when he took on himself the vows of a Christian.

To manage the affairs of a family as large as that of which Mrs. Brown had the charge, to provide for them, and attend to the education of her children, was no light task. She felt the burden, and was fully aware of the importance of the trust which, in the providence of God, had been placed in her hands. Part of a letter to a brother-in-law, to whom she looked for advice, and on whose judgment she relied very much, exhibits her anxieties and her support at this period. It bears date, August 10th, 1819.

Dear Brother,—Although I have been expecting a letter from you for some time, I have failed to receive it. I am often at a loss for your advice, but the distance is such, and the way of obtaining it by letter so uncertain, that I am often obliged to exercise my own judgment. I very much miss James and the girls who are at school, but the latter will soon be at home, and will be company and a comfort to me in my bereaved and lonely pilgrimage. The loss of one of the best of husbands is a trial that requires the support of the religion of Christ.

When I remember, however, that his warfare is over, that he has entered into the full enjoyment of God, and that it is to last forever, I am filled with comfort. for the continued support of the everlasting gospel! *'Though he slay me, yet will I trust in him.'* Dear brother, when difficulties present themselves like mountains, I find great comfort in that text—*'Leave thy fatherless children; I will preserve them alive, and let thy widows trust in me.'* This is the promise of the Almighty, and have I not been an object of his peculiar care? Robbed of my parents when quite small, his providence has brought me thus far, and his mighty arm is able to sustain me under any trial. for that faith in constant exercise, that works by love, and purifies the heart.

The God in whom she expressed such confident trust gave her strength equal to her day. Blessed with health, attending diligently and cheerfully to the interests committed to her care, she passed the years of her widowhood, until it became manifest in 1823, that the hand of serious disease was on her. In the meantime, her second daughter had been married to the Rev. James Morrison, who succeeded her husband as pastor of New Providence congregation, and was one of the great sources of her comfort in the last years of her life. Her oldest son having finished his collegiate course, had been received under the care of Lexington Presbytery, and was at home aiding in the care of the family, and pursuing his studies under the direction of the late Rev. George A. Baxter, D. D., at that time president of Washington College.

It was in the summer of 1823 that the health of Mrs. Brown began to fail. In the autumn of that year it became manifest that disease had fixed itself upon her, and the winter passed in the insidious progress of pulmonary consumption, while every means was unavailingly used to arrest it. To no one did it become manifest sooner than to herself, that the sickness was unto death. She expressed her conviction as to the issue, long before her family and friends had abandoned hope in her case; but to gratify them, she continued to use means to counteract the workings of disease, long after she was fully convinced that they were entirely ineffectual. In no part of her course did her character and piety shine more brightly. She was not only calm, she was cheerful, and was sustained to the end by Him who hath said, "*I will never leave thee nor forsake thee.*"

And yet there were considerations arising from the state of her family that were calculated to put her faith to a severe trial. Her maternal anxieties were particularly directed to the youngest four of her children. In the latter part of February she called her oldest son into her chamber, telling him that it was her wish to settle some family matters. She then said it was useless for her family to conceal from themselves that which was perfectly manifest to her, that she was steadily sinking, and could not live much longer. She said she had no fear of death, and her only wish was to have some plan fixed for disposing of the four younger children; expressing at the same time her entire comfort in committing them into the hands of God, that they were the children of the covenant, and the God of their fathers would take care of them.

In the course of a few days this was arranged to her entire satisfaction. They were to live with their brother-in-law, and into his and their sister's hands she solemnly committed them, and dismissed all worldly cares from her mind. About the same time she directed that a neat pocket Bible should be purchased for each of her children, and presented as the legacy of their dying mother. This occurred nearly two months before her death, and it is not recollected by any of her family that she spoke on any subject connected with worldly matters after this.

There is nothing witnessed on earth which has more of the moral sublime in it, than the Christian, in the full exercise of his intellectual powers, perfectly aware of what his condition is, watching his own progress to the entrance of the dark valley. The testimony of God and the promise of Christ are his only, but his all-sufficient support—his ground of hope and joy. Knowing in whom he has believed, and that He is able to take care of all that has been committed to him, that he is faithful and will do it, instead of shrinking from the meeting, he cheerfully holds out the hand to welcome death, not to him the king of terrors, but the messenger of his heavenly Father, sent to release him from a state of warfare and sin, and introduce him to the rest that remaineth for the people of God.

To witness such a scene is a high privilege, and such was witnessed in the death of Mrs. Brown. Her friends were allowed the privilege of being informed of all the exercises of her mind, as step by step disease moved her forward, till she passed into the darkness of the transit from earth into the city, where "*there is no night, and they need no candle, neither light of the sun, for the Lord God giveth them light.*"

In the last weeks of her life, her sufferings were not intensely severe. For only a short time was it necessary to watch by her bed. The 18th of April, 1824, was a communion Sabbath in New Providence. Until Friday she had spoken with ease, and conversed freely with all friends who called to see her. But at that time it became a labour for her to talk, and she seemed not disposed to converse with anyone. Her family were aware that this distinctly marked one stage in her disease; that it would pass away and be succeeded by the power to talk with ease and a disposition to converse, and then in a short time, possibly in a few hours, certainly in a few days at most, all suffering would end with her forever.

It was in the latter part of the night of Tuesday, the 20th, that the difficulty in speaking passed away, and she then knew the end was near. The meeting of Lexington Presbytery was to take place on Thursday, and it was expected that her oldest son would be licensed to preach the gospel during that meeting. About this event she had felt much interest. It seemed to be her last wish concerning the things of earth to see him enter on the work of the ministry. On Wednesday morning, soon after breakfast, she inquired of him whether he was preparing to start to Presbytery, as she knew it would be necessary for him to set off that forenoon to reach the place in time. He told her he did not wish to leave her, and was not going.

She at once expressed her decided wish that he should go, saying that she might live till his return, and if she did not, it would be a greater comfort to her to know that he was gone to receive his licensure, than to have him stay with her. She then directed that the servants first, and then her children, should be called in, that she might take leave of them. To each she gave some words of counsel and exhortation, again committed the four youngest to those who had undertaken to supply her place when she was gone, invoked the blessing of God on all, and then felt she had nothing more to do but to die.

Through this solemn, touching scene, while every other cheek was wet with tears, she alone was perfectly composed. With the fullness of tranquil Christian hope she felt it her privilege to adopt the language of the apostle, *"The time of my departure is at hand. I have fought a good fight, I have finished my course, I have kept the faith: henceforth there is laid up for me a crown of righteousness, which the Lord, the righteous Judge, shall give me at that day."*

On Friday, between three and four o'clock, p. m., her son was licensed to preach the gospel in the church of Mossy Creek, a distance of about forty miles from his mother, and immediately set off for home. He had heard nothing from her after leaving her on Wednesday. If she had died any time before Thursday noon, he knew she must be buried before his return. When he came to the residences of the families from whom he could expect to get any intelligence respecting his mother, they had gone to bed, and of course he could hear nothing. But there was one spot which he knew would give him some information before he reached home.

His road led him past the church, and the graveyard would show whether it had received another tenant since he had passed it. His approach to it was at the end opposite that in which his mother's grave would be: there was no moonlight, and as he drew near he endeavoured to strain his sight through the darkness, and learn the state of the case. It was not until he rode up to the enclosure, only a few yards from his father's grave, that he could see plainly the ground had not been disturbed there. It was then certain that his mother was not dead on the morning of that day, and hope whispered he might still find her alive. He had about three miles to ride, and spurring on his jaded horse the distance was soon passed over.

It was a few minutes before one o'clock that he dropped the saddle-bags off his arm in the hall, and opened the door that led into his mother's room. He found her unable to speak, though she had spoken quite intelligibly less than half an hour before. But it was noticed by those in the room, that when the door was opened, she turned her eyes in that direction, and fixing them on him, followed him as he approached her bedside. In about two hours after this she ceased to breathe, and her ransomed spirit passed into that world,

Where the saints of all ages in harmony meet,
Their Saviour and brethren transported to greet;
While the anthems of rapture unceasingly roll,

And the smile of the Lord is the feast of the soul.

On the forenoon of the following Sabbath, her remains were placed beside those of her husband, and her son went from the grave of his mother into the pulpit, which had been occupied by his father, and preached his first sermon. Few men commence the work of the ministry in circumstances so solemn, so deeply affecting as those in which he was placed. He has often expressed the opinion that his mother's prayers placed him in the pulpit. Contrary to his father's plans for his course in life, and contrary to his own plans, the providence of God made the path of duty very plain, when the time came for him to decide to what his life should be devoted, and this decision accorded with the cherished desire of his mother.

Mary Moore was a small woman, slender, and delicate in her person. Her usual weight was about one hundred pounds. The only remarkable feature in her face was the large, prominent eyes, which were a light blue. Her forehead was broad and rather square. No exposure could produce freckles on her cheeks, or change her complexion. It is said that in her youth she was thought to be handsome; but her chief ornament then, and through life, was a meek and quiet spirit, which, in the sight of the Lord, is of great price. The period at which she became pious is not known, but most probably it was before the breaking up of her father's family; and if so, it must have been before she was ten years of age.

CHAPTER 11

God's Faithfulness

It is now (1854) more than thirty years since Mary Moore closed her eventful life, and left her young family orphans. These years have not passed away without working their changes. The seed that was sown has been springing up, and bringing forth fruit. Without detailing the steps in the progress of events, some of the results will be briefly presented.

Of the seven sons of the little captive girl, five have entered the ministry in the Presbyterian church, and one has been for several years a ruling elder in the congregation of which his father was the pastor. The youngest son studied medicine, and settled at Russelville, in Tennessee, where he resided until his death in 1851. He was eminent in his profession. It was said of him in the brief obituary notice, "The widow, the orphan, and the poor will long remember him with gratitude." He met death sustained by the same faith which had cheered his mother, and none who were acquainted with him doubt that he has gone to join her in the kingdom of heaven. The third daughter died in early youth, after having given satisfactory evidence that she had made her peace with God.

She had lived for some years in Rogersville, Tennessee, with her elder sister, Lavinia, the wife of Dr. William A. Walker. Her health never had been vigorous, and she was the first of the family that was called to follow the parents to the land where "the weary are at rest." All Mary's grandchildren, who have arrived at the age of mature life, are members of the Presbyterian church; two of her grand-daughters have married Presbyterian ministers, and three of her grandsons are preparing to enter the ministry in the same church.

The question has been asked sometimes, "To what are we to attribute this marked and happy result in this family?" Perhaps it never can be satisfactorily answered. The only answer may be, "Even so, Father, for so it seemed good in thy sight." But so far as second causes are concerned, there are some considerations which it may not be amiss to mention, as tending to the solution of this question.

Mr. and Mrs. Brown did not bring up their children for this world. In their whole intercourse with their family, they made it evident to them that their great and ever present concern was that their children should serve God. They did not neglect to attend to their worldly interests, but they were careful to set before them in their daily walk, and in all their conversation, the infinite importance of serving God, and the comparative unimportance of all the wealth and honours of this world. The father once said to one of the beloved elders of his church, in the hearing of his oldest son, then quite a youth, without knowing that the remark was heard by him, "I have no wish that my children should be wealthy, or rise to places of worldly distinction; but it is the ever anxious desire of my heart that they shall be pious, and consecrate themselves to God's service, and I daily feel that I can trust him to provide for them."

Several years after the date of this conversation, he had serious thoughts of removing westward to the region bordering on the Mississippi, and visited that section of country. After his return, in assigning the reasons that determined his mind not to remove there, he said that he was not willing to bring up his family in the state of morals which existed in that region, and run the risk to which his children would be exposed. These incidents indicate distinctly what his views were. The views of the mother and father perfectly coincided. To the oldest son she once said, when urging on him the claims of God for the affections of his heart, and the service of his life, "Ever since we have had any children, your father and I have often kneeled by your bed when you were asleep, and solemnly dedicated you to God and his service."

This feeling thus expressed by both parents, was carried out in their whole course of action toward their children, and for them; and there can be no doubt that much of the future result is to be attributed to this.

The death of the father while most of the children were quite young, devolved on the mother the duty of attending to their education for several years, and most faithfully did she discharge it. An extract from a sermon on the subject of education, delivered before the Lexington Presbytery by a member of that body, in which allusion is made to her, may be introduced here as illustrating this point.

I was once acquainted with an eminently pious mother, who was left a widow with a family of ten children, the oldest only nineteen years of age. Soon after her husband's death, she had the pleasure of seeing some of the oldest unite themselves with the church of Christ. Her own health soon failed, and it became evident that she had almost finished her course on earth. No one discovered this sooner than she did herself. For at least a year previous to her death she often conversed freely with her friends on the subject. She was calm and composed. Death had no terror to her. She knew that if her earthly house of this tabernacle were dissolved, she had a building of God, an house not made with hands, eternal in the heavens.

But whilst she had no anxiety for herself, her heart yearned with all the strength of maternal tenderness over her children, soon to be left in this world of sin and temptation without either father or mother. She often talked to me on this subject with the tears flowing over her pale cheeks. She never expressed the least desire that her children might possess the riches, the honours, or the pleasures of this world; but she did express the most earnest anxiety that they might be well educated, brought up in the fear of God, and become true Christians, glorify God on earth, and be prepared for heaven.

I have every reason to know that she ceased not to pray for her children as long as she had breath. One of the most affecting scenes I ever witnessed took place three or four days before her death. When she found that her strength was fast failing, and that the time of her departure was at hand, she caused her servants to be called around her bed, gave them her dying counsel, suited to the character and age of each, and then bade them farewell. After this she had her children called to her, beginning with the oldest, and most solemnly and affectionately counselled and exhorted them to serve the Lord God of their fathers, and then looking on the four youngest with inexpressible tenderness, first committed them to her covenant-keeping God, and then to those who had promised her that as far as God would enable them, they would act toward them the part of earthly parents.

She directed that a Bible should be given to each of them as a legacy from their mother. I saw that mother die. Her end was peace. Her departure was like the sun setting in a clear summer evening, calm, peaceful, beautiful, glorious. I have lived to see all her children members of the church, five of them ministers of the gospel, one a valuable elder in the church, and all I trust following her footsteps to heaven. I need not tell some who hear me who that mother was.

When she was taken away, and that which she had so wisely commenced and so faithfully attended to devolved on the Rev. Mr. Morrison and his wife, it was carried on in the same spirit. The younger children of the family owe very much to them.

Another thing which deserves notice from the influence which it exerted in this matter, is the character of the community in which this family grew up. Of the population composing the congregation of New Providence, it may be said with truth, that a more orderly, pious population can hardly be found in the United States. It has been so from the first settlement of that section of the country. It is a plain, intelligent, contented community. Not much of wealth has ever existed amongst them, and still less of poverty. They have lived in the possession of comfortable independence, with very little anxiety for anything more. From a very early period they have been blessed with an able ministry. The consequence of all these influences has been, that the gathering of whole families into the communion of the church has not been an unfrequent thing in that congregation.

In this community where there was so little to counteract, and so much to enforce the influence of the instruction given to this family, and of the example set before them, it was their happy lot to spend the first years of their lives, and form their characters. The result is not surprising. In many other cases where there may be unquestioned, and even ardent piety in the parents, there is seen in their conduct a marked and eager grasping after the things of this world, and in their conversation before their children an importance is attached to them, which fills the youthful mind with false ideas of their value, and fixes the desires on them so inordinately, that they are not likely to seek first the kingdom of God and his righteousness.

And where there is no defect, either in parental instruction or example, other pernicious influences may be brought to bear with ruinous effect, while the moral character is forming for future life and for eternity. "*Lot dwelled in the cities of the plain, and pitched his tent towards*

Sodom. But the men of Sodom were wicked, and sinners before the Lord ex-ceedingly." And while his righteous soul was vexed with the filthy conversation of the wicked, his children were brought up in this ungodly society. The deplorable result is seen in the disastrous history of his family. And in numberless instances in this day, similar consequences are seen to the unspeakable grief of pious parents, and the scandal of the church of God.

Parents who, for the sake of worldly advantages, place their families in the midst of prevailing ungodliness, and as is too often the case, where they are deprived of the advantages of the faithful preaching of the gospel, and exposed to the constant influence of wicked associates, are endangering the souls of their children in a fearful degree. It is no wonderful thing if they live in sin, become scoffers at sacred things, and pierce with many sorrows the souls of those who have placed them in the midst of strong and constant temptations. There are no promises more explicit than those annexed to the covenant, "*I will be a God to thee, and to thy seed after thee.*" But to secure the blessings, parents must pursue the course of conduct which always points to them, and is calculated to lay hold of them.

In 1849 one of the sons of this family visited Abb's Valley. Part of a letter written after his return forms not an unsuitable conclusion to the tale recorded in the foregoing pages. "While I was with our relations in the Valley, I counted up the descendants of the three children of our grandfather. There are one hundred and sixteen now living, (as st time of first publication). Most of the grandchildren who have come to the years of mature life are members of the church, giving pleasing evidence of piety. my brother, may we not look on this as in answer to the prayers of our grandmother, when amidst the flames she committed the little remnant of her murdered family to a covenant-keeping God? And how much richer is the legacy to her descendants than all the world beside!

> *My boast is not that I deduce my birth*
> *From loins enthroned, and rulers of the earth;*
> *But higher far my proud pretensions rise,*
> *The son of parents passed into the skies.*"

LEONAUR

ALSO FROM LEONAUR
AVAILABLE IN SOFTCOVER OR HARDCOVER WITH DUST JACKET

A HISTORY OF THE FRENCH & INDIAN WAR *by Arthur G. Bradley*—The Seven Years War as it was fought in the New World has always fascinated students of military history—here is the story of that confrontation.

WASHINGTON'S EARLY CAMPAIGNS *by James Hadden*—The French Post Expedition, Great Meadows and Braddock's Defeat—including Braddock's Orderly Books.

BOUQUET & THE OHIO INDIAN WAR *by Cyrus Cort & William Smith*—Two Accounts of the Campaigns of 1763-1764: Bouquet's Campaigns by Cyrus Cort & The History of Bouquet's Expeditions by William Smith.

NARRATIVES OF THE FRENCH & INDIAN WAR: 2 *by David Holden, Samuel Jenks, Lemuel Lyon, Mary Cochrane Rogers & Henry T. Blake*—Contains The Diary of Sergeant David Holden, Captain Samuel Jenks' Journal, The Journal of Lemuel Lyon, Journal of a French Officer at the Siege of Quebec, A Battle Fought on Snowshoes & The Battle of Lake George.

NARRATIVES OF THE FRENCH & INDIAN WAR *by Brown, Eastburn, Hawks & Putnam*—Ranger Brown's Narrative, The Adventures of Robert Eastburn, The Journal of Rufus Putnam—Provincial Infantry & Orderly Book and Journal of Major John Hawks on the Ticonderoga-Crown Point Campaign.

THE 7TH (QUEEN'S OWN) HUSSARS: Volume 1—1688-1792 *by C. R. B. Barrett*—As Dragoons During the Flanders Campaign, War of the Austrian Succession and the Seven Years War.

INDIA'S FREE LANCES *by H. G. Keene*—European Mercenary Commanders in Hindustan 1770-1820.

THE BENGAL EUROPEAN REGIMENT *by P. R. Innes*—An Elite Regiment of the Honourable East India Company 1756-1858.

MUSKET & TOMAHAWK *by Francis Parkman*—A Military History of the French & Indian War, 1753-1760.

THE BLACK WATCH AT TICONDEROGA *by Frederick B. Richards*—Campaigns in the French & Indian War.

QUEEN'S RANGERS *by Frederick B. Richards*—John Simcoe and his Rangers During the Revolutionary War for America.

LEONAUR

ALSO FROM LEONAUR
AVAILABLE IN SOFTCOVER OR HARDCOVER WITH DUST JACKET

JOURNALS OF ROBERT ROGERS OF THE RANGERS *by Robert Rogers*—The exploits of Rogers & the Rangers in his own words during 1755-1761 in the French & Indian War.

GALLOPING GUNS *by James Young*—The Experiences of an Officer of the Bengal Horse Artillery During the Second Maratha War 1804-1805.

GORDON *by Demetrius Charles Boulger*—The Career of Gordon of Khartoum.

THE BATTLE OF NEW ORLEANS *by Zachary F. Smith*—The final major engagement of the War of 1812.

THE TWO WARS OF MRS DUBERLY *by Frances Isabella Duberly*—An Intrepid Victorian Lady's Experience of the Crimea and Indian Mutiny.

WITH THE GUARDS' BRIGADE DURING THE BOER WAR *by Edward P. Lowry*—On Campaign from Bloemfontein to Koomati Poort and Back.

THE REBELLIOUS DUCHESS *by Paul F. S. Dermoncourt*—The Adventures of the Duchess of Berri and Her Attempt to Overthrow French Monarchy.

MEN OF THE MUTINY *by John Tulloch Nash & Henry Metcalfe*—Two Accounts of the Great Indian Mutiny of 1857: Fighting with the Bengal Yeomanry Cavalry & Private Metcalfe at Lucknow.

CAMPAIGN IN THE CRIMEA *by George Shuldham Peard*—The Recollections of an Officer of the 20th Regiment of Foot.

WITHIN SEBASTOPOL *by K. Hodasevich*—A Narrative of the Campaign in the Crimea, and of the Events of the Siege.

WITH THE CAVALRY TO AFGHANISTAN *by William Taylor*—The Experiences of a Trooper of H. M. 4th Light Dragoons During the First Afghan War.

THE CAWNPORE MAN *by Mowbray Thompson*—A First Hand Account of the Siege and Massacre During the Indian Mutiny By One of Four Survivors.

BRIGADE COMMANDER: AFGHANISTAN *by Henry Brooke*—The Journal of the Commander of the 2nd Infantry Brigade, Kandahar Field Force During the Second Afghan War.

BANCROFT OF THE BENGAL HORSE ARTILLERY *by N. W. Bancroft*—An Account of the First Sikh War 1845-1846.

LEONAUR

ALSO FROM LEONAUR
AVAILABLE IN SOFTCOVER OR HARDCOVER WITH DUST JACKET

AFGHANISTAN: THE BELEAGUERED BRIGADE *by G. R. Gleig*—An Account of Sale's Brigade During the First Afghan War.

IN THE RANKS OF THE C. I. V *by Erskine Childers*—With the City Imperial Volunteer Battery (Honourable Artillery Company) in the Second Boer War.

THE BENGAL NATIVE ARMY *by F. G. Cardew*—An Invaluable Reference Resource.

THE 7TH (QUEEN'S OWN) HUSSARS: Volume 4—1688-1914 *by C. R. B. Barrett*—Uniforms, Equipment, Weapons, Traditions, the Services of Notable Officers and Men & the Appendices to All Volumes—Volume 4: 1688-1914.

THE SWORD OF THE CROWN *by Eric W. Sheppard*—A History of the British Army to 1914.

THE 7TH (QUEEN'S OWN) HUSSARS: Volume 3—1818-1914 *by C. R. B. Barrett*—On Campaign During the Canadian Rebellion, the Indian Mutiny, the Sudan, Matabeleland, Mashonaland and the Boer War Volume 3: 1818-1914.

THE KHARTOUM CAMPAIGN *by Bennet Burleigh*—A Special Correspondent's View of the Reconquest of the Sudan by British and Egyptian Forces under Kitchener—1898.

EL PUCHERO *by Richard McSherry*—The Letters of a Surgeon of Volunteers During Scott's Campaign of the American-Mexican War 1847-1848.

RIFLEMAN SAHIB *by E. Maude*—The Recollections of an Officer of the Bombay Rifles During the Southern Mahratta Campaign, Second Sikh War, Persian Campaign and Indian Mutiny.

THE KING'S HUSSAR *by Edwin Mole*—The Recollections of a 14th (King's) Hussar During the Victorian Era.

JOHN COMPANY'S CAVALRYMAN *by William Johnson*—The Experiences of a British Soldier in the Crimea, the Persian Campaign and the Indian Mutiny.

COLENSO & DURNFORD'S ZULU WAR *by Frances E. Colenso & Edward Durnford*—The first and possibly the most important history of the Zulu War.

U. S. DRAGOON *by Samuel E. Chamberlain*—Experiences in the Mexican War 1846-48 and on the South Western Frontier.

LEONAUR

ALSO FROM LEONAUR
AVAILABLE IN SOFTCOVER OR HARDCOVER WITH DUST JACKET

THE 2ND MAORI WAR: 1860-1861 *by Robert Carey*—The Second Maori War, or First Taranaki War, one more bloody instalment of the conflicts between European settlers and the indigenous Maori people.

A JOURNAL OF THE SECOND SIKH WAR *by Daniel A. Sandford*—The Experiences of an Ensign of the 2nd Bengal European Regiment During the Campaign in the Punjab, India, 1848-49.

THE LIGHT INFANTRY OFFICER *by John H. Cooke*—The Experiences of an Officer of the 43rd Light Infantry in America During the War of 1812.

BUSHVELDT CARBINEERS *by George Witton*—The War Against the Boers in South Africa and the 'Breaker' Morant Incident.

LAKE'S CAMPAIGNS IN INDIA *by Hugh Pearse*—The Second Anglo Maratha War, 1803-1807.

BRITAIN IN AFGHANISTAN 1: THE FIRST AFGHAN WAR 1839-42 *by Archibald Forbes*—From invasion to destruction-a British military disaster.

BRITAIN IN AFGHANISTAN 2: THE SECOND AFGHAN WAR 1878-80 *by Archibald Forbes*—This is the history of the Second Afghan War-another episode of British military history typified by savagery, massacre, siege and battles.

UP AMONG THE PANDIES *by Vivian Dering Majendie*—Experiences of a British Officer on Campaign During the Indian Mutiny, 1857-1858.

MUTINY: 1857 *by James Humphries*—Authentic Voices from the Indian Mutiny-First Hand Accounts of Battles, Sieges and Personal Hardships.

BLOW THE BUGLE, DRAW THE SWORD *by W. H. G. Kingston*—The Wars, Campaigns, Regiments and Soldiers of the British & Indian Armies During the Victorian Era, 1839-1898.

WAR BEYOND THE DRAGON PAGODA *by Major J. J. Snodgrass*—A Personal Narrative of the First Anglo-Burmese War 1824 - 1826.

THE HERO OF ALIWAL *by James Humphries*—The Campaigns of Sir Harry Smith in India, 1843-1846, During the Gwalior War & the First Sikh War.

ALL FOR A SHILLING A DAY *by Donald F. Featherstone*—The story of H.M. 16th, the Queen's Lancers During the first Sikh War 1845-1846.

LEONAUR

ALSO FROM LEONAUR
AVAILABLE IN SOFTCOVER OR HARDCOVER WITH DUST JACKET

THE FALL OF THE MOGHUL EMPIRE OF HINDUSTAN *by H. G. Keene*—
By the beginning of the nineteenth century, as British and Indian armies under Lake and Wellesley dominated the scene, a little over half a century of conflict brought the Moghul Empire to its knees.

LADY SALE'S AFGHANISTAN *by Florentia Sale*—An Indomitable Victorian Lady's Account of the Retreat from Kabul During the First Afghan War.

THE CAMPAIGN OF MAGENTA AND SOLFERINO 1859 *by Harold Carmichael Wylly*—The Decisive Conflict for the Unification of Italy.

FRENCH'S CAVALRY CAMPAIGN *by J. G. Maydon*—A Special Correspondent's View of British Army Mounted Troops During the Boer War.

CAVALRY AT WATERLOO *by Sir Evelyn Wood*—British Mounted Troops During the Campaign of 1815.

THE SUBALTERN *by George Robert Gleig*—The Experiences of an Officer of the 85th Light Infantry During the Peninsular War.

NAPOLEON AT BAY, 1814 *by F. Loraine Petre*—The Campaigns to the Fall of the First Empire.

NAPOLEON AND THE CAMPAIGN OF 1806 *by Colonel Vachée*—The Napoleonic Method of Organisation and Command to the Battles of Jena & Auerstädt.

THE COMPLETE ADVENTURES IN THE CONNAUGHT RANGERS *by William Grattan*—The 88th Regiment during the Napoleonic Wars by a Serving Officer.

BUGLER AND OFFICER OF THE RIFLES *by William Green & Harry Smith*—With the 95th (Rifles) during the Peninsular & Waterloo Campaigns of the Napoleonic Wars.

NAPOLEONIC WAR STORIES *by Sir Arthur Quiller-Couch*—Tales of soldiers, spies, battles & sieges from the Peninsular & Waterloo campaingns.

CAPTAIN OF THE 95TH (RIFLES) *by Jonathan Leach*—An officer of Wellington's sharpshooters during the Peninsular, South of France and Waterloo campaigns of the Napoleonic wars.

RIFLEMAN COSTELLO *by Edward Costello*—The adventures of a soldier of the 95th (Rifles) in the Peninsular & Waterloo Campaigns of the Napoleonic wars.

LEONAUR

ALSO FROM LEONAUR
AVAILABLE IN SOFTCOVER OR HARDCOVER WITH DUST JACKET

AT THEM WITH THE BAYONET *by Donald F. Featherstone*—The first Anglo-Sikh War 1845-1846.

STEPHEN CRANE'S BATTLES *by Stephen Crane*—Nine Decisive Battles Recounted by the Author of 'The Red Badge of Courage'.

THE GURKHA WAR *by H. T. Prinsep*—The Anglo-Nepalese Conflict in North East India 1814-1816.

FIRE & BLOOD *by G. R. Gleig*—The burning of Washington & the battle of New Orleans, 1814, through the eyes of a young British soldier.

SOUND ADVANCE! *by Joseph Anderson*—Experiences of an officer of HM 50th regiment in Australia, Burma & the Gwalior war.

THE CAMPAIGN OF THE INDUS *by Thomas Holdsworth*—Experiences of a British Officer of the 2nd (Queen's Royal) Regiment in the Campaign to Place Shah Shuja on the Throne of Afghanistan 1838 - 1840.

WITH THE MADRAS EUROPEAN REGIMENT IN BURMA *by John Butler*—The Experiences of an Officer of the Honourable East India Company's Army During the First Anglo-Burmese War 1824 - 1826.

IN ZULULAND WITH THE BRITISH ARMY *by Charles L. Norris-Newman*—The Anglo-Zulu war of 1879 through the first-hand experiences of a special correspondent.

BESIEGED IN LUCKNOW *by Martin Richard Gubbins*—The first Anglo-Sikh War 1845-1846.

A TIGER ON HORSEBACK *by L. March Phillips*—The Experiences of a Trooper & Officer of Rimington's Guides - The Tigers - during the Anglo-Boer war 1899 - 1902.

SEPOYS, SIEGE & STORM *by Charles John Griffiths*—The Experiences of a young officer of H.M.'s 61st Regiment at Ferozepore, Delhi ridge and at the fall of Delhi during the Indian mutiny 1857.

CAMPAIGNING IN ZULULAND *by W. E. Montague*—Experiences on campaign during the Zulu war of 1879 with the 94th Regiment.

THE STORY OF THE GUIDES *by G.J. Younghusband*—The Exploits of the Soldiers of the famous Indian Army Regiment from the northwest frontier 1847 - 1900.

LEONAUR

ALSO FROM LEONAUR
AVAILABLE IN SOFTCOVER OR HARDCOVER WITH DUST JACKET

ZULU:1879 *by D.C.F. Moodie & the Leonaur Editors*—The Anglo-Zulu War of 1879 from contemporary sources: First Hand Accounts, Interviews, Dispatches, Official Documents & Newspaper Reports.

THE RED DRAGOON *by W.J. Adams*—With the 7th Dragoon Guards in the Cape of Good Hope against the Boers & the Kaffir tribes during the 'war of the axe' 1843-48'.

THE RECOLLECTIONS OF SKINNER OF SKINNER'S HORSE *by James Skinner*—James Skinner and his 'Yellow Boys' Irregular cavalry in the wars of India between the British, Mahratta, Rajput, Mogul, Sikh & Pindarree Forces.

A CAVALRY OFFICER DURING THE SEPOY REVOLT *by A. R. D. Mackenzie*—Experiences with the 3rd Bengal Light Cavalry, the Guides and Sikh Irregular Cavalry from the outbreak to Delhi and Lucknow.

A NORFOLK SOLDIER IN THE FIRST SIKH WAR *by J W Baldwin*—Experiences of a private of H.M. 9th Regiment of Foot in the battles for the Punjab, India 1845-6.

TOMMY ATKINS' WAR STORIES: 14 FIRST HAND ACCOUNTS—Fourteen first hand accounts from the ranks of the British Army during Queen Victoria's Empire.

THE WATERLOO LETTERS *by H. T. Siborne*—Accounts of the Battle by British Officers for its Foremost Historian.

NEY: GENERAL OF CAVALRY VOLUME 1—1769-1799 *by Antoine Bulos*—The Early Career of a Marshal of the First Empire.

NEY: MARSHAL OF FRANCE VOLUME 2—1799-1805 *by Antoine Bulos*—The Early Career of a Marshal of the First Empire.

AIDE-DE-CAMP TO NAPOLEON *by Philippe-Paul de Ségur*—For anyone interested in the Napoleonic Wars this book, written by one who was intimate with the strategies and machinations of the Emperor, will be essential reading.

TWILIGHT OF EMPIRE *by Sir Thomas Ussher & Sir George Cockburn*—Two accounts of Napoleon's Journeys in Exile to Elba and St. Helena: Narrative of Events by Sir Thomas Ussher & Napoleon's Last Voyage: Extract of a diary by Sir George Cockburn.

PRIVATE WHEELER *by William Wheeler*—The letters of a soldier of the 51st Light Infantry during the Peninsular War & at Waterloo.

LEONAUR

ALSO FROM LEONAUR

AVAILABLE IN SOFTCOVER OR HARDCOVER WITH DUST JACKET

OFFICERS & GENTLEMEN *by Peter Hawker & William Graham*—Two Accounts of British Officers During the Peninsula War: Officer of Light Dragoons by Peter Hawker & Campaign in Portugal and Spain by William Graham .

THE WALCHEREN EXPEDITION *by Anonymous*—The Experiences of a British Officer of the 81st Regt. During the Campaign in the Low Countries of 1809.

LADIES OF WATERLOO *by Charlotte A. Eaton, Magdalene de Lancey & Juana Smith*—The Experiences of Three Women During the Campaign of 1815: Waterloo Days by Charlotte A. Eaton, A Week at Waterloo by Magdalene de Lancey & Juana's Story by Juana Smith.

JOURNAL OF AN OFFICER IN THE KING'S GERMAN LEGION *by John Frederick Hering*—Recollections of Campaigning During the Napoleonic Wars.

JOURNAL OF AN ARMY SURGEON IN THE PENINSULAR WAR *by Charles Boutflower*—The Recollections of a British Army Medical Man on Campaign During the Napoleonic Wars.

ON CAMPAIGN WITH MOORE AND WELLINGTON *by Anthony Hamilton*—The Experiences of a Soldier of the 43rd Regiment During the Peninsular War.

THE ROAD TO AUSTERLITZ *by R. G. Burton*—Napoleon's Campaign of 1805.

SOLDIERS OF NAPOLEON *by A. J. Doisy De Villargennes & Arthur Chuquet*—The Experiences of the Men of the French First Empire: Under the Eagles by A. J. Doisy De Villargennes & Voices of 1812 by Arthur Chuquet .

INVASION OF FRANCE, 1814 *by F. W. O. Maycock*—The Final Battles of the Napoleonic First Empire.

LEIPZIG—A CONFLICT OF TITANS *by Frederic Shoberl*—A Personal Experience of the 'Battle of the Nations' During the Napoleonic Wars, October 14th-19th, 1813.

SLASHERS *by Charles Cadell*—The Campaigns of the 28th Regiment of Foot During the Napoleonic Wars by a Serving Officer.

BATTLE IMPERIAL *by Charles William Vane*—The Campaigns in Germany & France for the Defeat of Napoleon 1813-1814.

SWIFT & BOLD *by Gibbes Rigaud*—The 60th Rifles During the Peninsula War.

LEONAUR

ALSO FROM LEONAUR
AVAILABLE IN SOFTCOVER OR HARDCOVER WITH DUST JACKET

ADVENTURES OF A YOUNG RIFLEMAN *by Johann Christian Maempel*—The Experiences of a Saxon in the French & British Armies During the Napoleonic Wars.

THE HUSSAR *by Norbert Landsheit & G. R. Gleig*—A German Cavalryman in British Service Throughout the Napoleonic Wars.

RECOLLECTIONS OF THE PENINSULA *by Moyle Sherer*—An Officer of the 34th Regiment of Foot—'The Cumberland Gentlemen'—on Campaign Against Napoleon's French Army in Spain.

MARINE OF REVOLUTION & CONSULATE *by Moreau de Jonnès*—The Recollections of a French Soldier of the Revolutionary Wars 1791-1804.

GENTLEMEN IN RED *by John Dobbs & Robert Knowles*—Two Accounts of British Infantry Officers During the Peninsular War Recollections of an Old 52nd Man by John Dobbs An Officer of Fusiliers by Robert Knowles.

CORPORAL BROWN'S CAMPAIGNS IN THE LOW COUNTRIES *by Robert Brown*—Recollections of a Coldstream Guard in the Early Campaigns Against Revolutionary France 1793-1795.

THE 7TH (QUEENS OWN) HUSSARS: Volume 2—1793-1815 *by C. R. B. Barrett*—During the Campaigns in the Low Countries & the Peninsula and Waterloo Campaigns of the Napoleonic Wars. Volume 2: 1793-1815.

THE MARENGO CAMPAIGN 1800 *by Herbert H. Sargent*—The Victory that Completed the Austrian Defeat in Italy.

DONALDSON OF THE 94TH—SCOTS BRIGADE *by Joseph Donaldson*—The Recollections of a Soldier During the Peninsula & South of France Campaigns of the Napoleonic Wars.

A CONSCRIPT FOR EMPIRE *by Philippe as told to Johann Christian Maempel*—The Experiences of a Young German Conscript During the Napoleonic Wars.

JOURNAL OF THE CAMPAIGN OF 1815 *by Alexander Cavalié Mercer*—The Experiences of an Officer of the Royal Horse Artillery During the Waterloo Campaign.

NAPOLEON'S CAMPAIGNS IN POLAND 1806-7 *by Robert Wilson*—The campaign in Poland from the Russian side of the conflict.

LEONAUR

ALSO FROM LEONAUR
AVAILABLE IN SOFTCOVER OR HARDCOVER WITH DUST JACKET

COLBORNE: A SINGULAR TALENT FOR WAR *by John Colborne*—The Napoleonic Wars Career of One of Wellington's Most Highly Valued Officers in Egypt, Holland, Italy, the Peninsula and at Waterloo.

NAPOLEON'S RUSSIAN CAMPAIGN *by Philippe Henri de Segur*—The Invasion, Battles and Retreat by an Aide-de-Camp on the Emperor's Staff.

WITH THE LIGHT DIVISION *by John H. Cooke*—The Experiences of an Officer of the 43rd Light Infantry in the Peninsula and South of France During the Napoleonic Wars.

WELLINGTON AND THE PYRENEES CAMPAIGN VOLUME I: FROM VITORIA TO THE BIDASSOA *by F. C. Beatson*—The final phase of the campaign in the Iberian Peninsula.

WELLINGTON AND THE INVASION OF FRANCE VOLUME II: THE BIDASSOA TO THE BATTLE OF THE NIVELLE *by F. C. Beatson*—The final phase of the campaign in the Iberian Peninsula.

WELLINGTON AND THE FALL OF FRANCE VOLUME III: THE GAVES AND THE BATTLE OF ORTHEZ *by F. C. Beatson*—The final phase of the campaign in the Iberian Peninsula.

NAPOLEON'S IMPERIAL GUARD: FROM MARENGO TO WATERLOO *by J. T. Headley*—The story of Napoleon's Imperial Guard and the men who commanded them.

BATTLES & SIEGES OF THE PENINSULAR WAR *by W. H. Fitchett*—Corunna, Busaco, Albuera, Ciudad Rodrigo, Badajos, Salamanca, San Sebastian & Others.

SERGEANT GUILLEMARD: THE MAN WHO SHOT NELSON? *by Robert Guillemard*—A Soldier of the Infantry of the French Army of Napoleon on Campaign Throughout Europe.

WITH THE GUARDS ACROSS THE PYRENEES *by Robert Batty*—The Experiences of a British Officer of Wellington's Army During the Battles for the Fall of Napoleonic France, 1813 .

A STAFF OFFICER IN THE PENINSULA *by E. W. Buckham*—An Officer of the British Staff Corps Cavalry During the Peninsula Campaign of the Napoleonic Wars.

THE LEIPZIG CAMPAIGN: 1813—NAPOLEON AND THE "BATTLE OF THE NATIONS" *by F. N. Maude*—Colonel Maude's analysis of Napoleon's campaign of 1813 around Leipzig.

LEONAUR

ALSO FROM LEONAUR
AVAILABLE IN SOFTCOVER OR HARDCOVER WITH DUST JACKET

BUGEAUD: A PACK WITH A BATON *by Thomas Robert Bugeaud*—The Early Campaigns of a Soldier of Napoleon's Army Who Would Become a Marshal of France.

WATERLOO RECOLLECTIONS *by Frederick Llewellyn*—Rare First Hand Accounts, Letters, Reports and Retellings from the Campaign of 1815.

SERGEANT NICOL *by Daniel Nicol*—The Experiences of a Gordon Highlander During the Napoleonic Wars in Egypt, the Peninsula and France.

THE JENA CAMPAIGN: 1806 *by F. N. Maude*—The Twin Battles of Jena & Auerstadt Between Napoleon's French and the Prussian Army.

PRIVATE O'NEIL *by Charles O'Neil*—The recollections of an Irish Rogue of H. M. 28th Regt.—The Slashers—during the Peninsula & Waterloo campaigns of the Napoleonic war.

ROYAL HIGHLANDER *by James Anton*—A soldier of H.M 42nd (Royal) Highlanders during the Peninsular, South of France & Waterloo Campaigns of the Napoleonic Wars.

CAPTAIN BLAZE *by Elzéar Blaze*—Life in Napoleons Army.

LEJEUNE VOLUME 1 *by Louis-François Lejeune*—The Napoleonic Wars through the Experiences of an Officer on Berthier's Staff.

LEJEUNE VOLUME 2 *by Louis-François Lejeune*—The Napoleonic Wars through the Experiences of an Officer on Berthier's Staff.

CAPTAIN COIGNET *by Jean-Roch Coignet*—A Soldier of Napoleon's Imperial Guard from the Italian Campaign to Russia and Waterloo.

FUSILIER COOPER *by John S. Cooper*—Experiences in the 7th (Royal) Fusiliers During the Peninsular Campaign of the Napoleonic Wars and the American Campaign to New Orleans.

FIGHTING NAPOLEON'S EMPIRE *by Joseph Anderson*—The Campaigns of a British Infantryman in Italy, Egypt, the Peninsular & the West Indies During the Napoleonic Wars.

CHASSEUR BARRES *by Jean-Baptiste Barres*—The experiences of a French Infantryman of the Imperial Guard at Austerlitz, Jena, Eylau, Friedland, in the Peninsular, Lutzen, Bautzen, Zinnwald and Hanau during the Napoleonic Wars.

LEONAUR

ALSO FROM LEONAUR
AVAILABLE IN SOFTCOVER OR HARDCOVER WITH DUST JACKET

CAPTAIN COIGNET *by Jean-Roch Coignet*—A Soldier of Napoleon's Imperial Guard from the Italian Campaign to Russia and Waterloo.

HUSSAR ROCCA *by Albert Jean Michel de Rocca*—A French cavalry officer's experiences of the Napoleonic Wars and his views on the Peninsular Campaigns against the Spanish, British And Guerilla Armies.

MARINES TO 95TH (RIFLES) *by Thomas Fernyhough*—The military experiences of Robert Fernyough during the Napoleonic Wars.

LIGHT BOB *by Robert Blakeney*—The experiences of a young officer in H.M 28th & 36th regiments of the British Infantry during the Peninsular Campaign of the Napoleonic Wars 1804 - 1814.

WITH WELLINGTON'S LIGHT CAVALRY *by William Tomkinson*—The Experiences of an officer of the 16th Light Dragoons in the Peninsular and Waterloo campaigns of the Napoleonic Wars.

SERGEANT BOURGOGNE *by Adrien Bourgogne*—With Napoleon's Imperial Guard in the Russian Campaign and on the Retreat from Moscow 1812 - 13.

SURTEES OF THE 95TH (RIFLES) *by William Surtees*—A Soldier of the 95th (Rifles) in the Peninsular campaign of the Napoleonic Wars.

SWORDS OF HONOUR *by Henry Newbolt & Stanley L. Wood*—The Careers of Six Outstanding Officers from the Napoleonic Wars, the Wars for India and the American Civil War.

ENSIGN BELL IN THE PENINSULAR WAR *by George Bell*—The Experiences of a young British Soldier of the 34th Regiment 'The Cumberland Gentlemen' in the Napoleonic wars.

HUSSAR IN WINTER *by Alexander Gordon*—A British Cavalry Officer during the retreat to Corunna in the Peninsular campaign of the Napoleonic Wars.

THE COMPLEAT RIFLEMAN HARRIS *by Benjamin Harris as told to and transcribed by Captain Henry Curling, 52nd Regt. of Foot*—The adventures of a soldier of the 95th (Rifles) during the Peninsular Campaign of the Napoleonic Wars.

THE ADVENTURES OF A LIGHT DRAGOON *by George Farmer & G.R. Gleig*—A cavalryman during the Peninsular & Waterloo Campaigns, in captivity & at the siege of Bhurtpore, India.

LEONAUR

ALSO FROM LEONAUR

AVAILABLE IN SOFTCOVER OR HARDCOVER WITH DUST JACKET

THE LIFE OF THE REAL BRIGADIER GERARD VOLUME 1—THE YOUNG HUSSAR 1782-1807 *by Jean-Baptiste De Marbot*—A French Cavalryman Of the Napoleonic Wars at Marengo, Austerlitz, Jena, Eylau & Friedland.

THE LIFE OF THE REAL BRIGADIER GERARD VOLUME 2—IMPERIAL AIDE-DE-CAMP 1807-1811 *by Jean-Baptiste De Marbot*—A French Cavalryman of the Napoleonic Wars at Saragossa, Landshut, Eckmuhl, Ratisbon, Aspern-Essling, Wagram, Busaco & Torres Vedras.

THE LIFE OF THE REAL BRIGADIER GERARD VOLUME 3—COLONEL OF CHASSEURS 1811-1815 *by Jean-Baptiste De Marbot*—A French Cavalryman in the retreat from Moscow, Lutzen, Bautzen, Katzbach, Leipzig, Hanau & Waterloo.

THE INDIAN WAR OF 1864 *by Eugene Ware*—The Experiences of a Young Officer of the 7th Iowa Cavalry on the Western Frontier During the Civil War.

THE MARCH OF DESTINY *by Charles E. Young & V. Devinny*—Dangers of the Trail in 1865 by Charles E. Young & The Story of a Pioneer by V. Devinny, two Accounts of Early Emigrants to Colorado.

CROSSING THE PLAINS *by William Audley Maxwell*—A First Hand Narrative of the Early Pioneer Trail to California in 1857.

CHIEF OF SCOUTS *by William F. Drannan*—A Pilot to Emigrant and Government Trains, Across the Plains of the Western Frontier.

THIRTY-ONE YEARS ON THE PLAINS AND IN THE MOUNTAINS *by William F. Drannan*—William Drannan was born to be a pioneer, hunter, trapper and wagon train guide during the momentous days of the Great American West.

THE INDIAN WARS VOLUNTEER *by William Thompson*—Recollections of the Conflict Against the Snakes, Shoshone, Bannocks, Modocs and Other Native Tribes of the American North West.

THE 4TH TENNESSEE CAVALRY *by George B. Guild*—The Services of Smith's Regiment of Confederate Cavalry by One of its Officers.

COLONEL WORTHINGTON'S SHILOH *by T. Worthington*—The Tennessee Campaign, 1862, by an Officer of the Ohio Volunteers.

FOUR YEARS IN THE SADDLE *by W. L. Curry*—The History of the First Regiment Ohio Volunteer Cavalry in the American Civil War.

LEONAUR

ALSO FROM LEONAUR
AVAILABLE IN SOFTCOVER OR HARDCOVER WITH DUST JACKET

LIFE IN THE ARMY OF NORTHERN VIRGINIA *by Carlton McCarthy*—The Observations of a Confederate Artilleryman of Cutshaw's Battalion During the American Civil War 1861-1865.

HISTORY OF THE CAVALRY OF THE ARMY OF THE POTOMAC *by Charles D. Rhodes*—Including Pope's Army of Virginia and the Cavalry Operations in West Virginia During the American Civil War.

CAMP-FIRE AND COTTON-FIELD *by Thomas W. Knox*—A New York Herald Correspondent's View of the American Civil War.

SERGEANT STILLWELL *by Leander Stillwell* —The Experiences of a Union Army Soldier of the 61st Illinois Infantry During the American Civil War.

STONEWALL'S CANNONEER *by Edward A. Moore*—Experiences with the Rockbridge Artillery, Confederate Army of Northern Virginia, During the American Civil War.

THE SIXTH CORPS *by George Stevens*—The Army of the Potomac, Union Army, During the American Civil War.

THE RAILROAD RAIDERS *by William Pittenger*—An Ohio Volunteers Recollections of the Andrews Raid to Disrupt the Confederate Railroad in Georgia During the American Civil War.

CITIZEN SOLDIER *by John Beatty*—An Account of the American Civil War by a Union Infantry Officer of Ohio Volunteers Who Became a Brigadier General.

COX: PERSONAL RECOLLECTIONS OF THE CIVIL WAR--VOLUME 1 *by Jacob Dolson Cox*—West Virginia, Kanawha Valley, Gauley Bridge, Cotton Mountain, South Mountain, Antietam, the Morgan Raid & the East Tennessee Campaign.

COX: PERSONAL RECOLLECTIONS OF THE CIVIL WAR--VOLUME 2 *by Jacob Dolson Cox*—Siege of Knoxville, East Tennessee, Atlanta Campaign, the Nashville Campaign & the North Carolina Campaign.

KERSHAW'S BRIGADE VOLUME 1 *by D. Augustus Dickert*—Manassas, Seven Pines, Sharpsburg (Antietam), Fredricksburg, Chancellorsville, Gettysburg, Chickamauga, Chattanooga, Fort Sanders & Bean Station.

KERSHAW'S BRIGADE VOLUME 2 *by D. Augustus Dickert*—At the wilderness, Cold Harbour, Petersburg, The Shenandoah Valley and Cedar Creek..

LEONAUR

ALSO FROM LEONAUR
AVAILABLE IN SOFTCOVER OR HARDCOVER WITH DUST JACKET

ESCAPE FROM THE FRENCH *by Edward Boys*—A Young Royal Navy Midshipman's Adventures During the Napoleonic War.

THE VOYAGE OF H.M.S. PANDORA *by Edward Edwards R. N. & George Hamilton, edited by Basil Thomson*—In Pursuit of the Mutineers of the Bounty in the South Seas—1790-1791.

MEDUSA *by J. B. Henry Savigny and Alexander Correard and Charlotte-Adélaïde Dard* —Narrative of a Voyage to Senegal in 1816 & The Sufferings of the Picard Family After the Shipwreck of the Medusa.

THE SEA WAR OF 1812 VOLUME 1 *by A. T. Mahan*—A History of the Maritime Conflict.

THE SEA WAR OF 1812 VOLUME 2 *by A. T. Mahan*—A History of the Maritime Conflict.

WETHERELL OF H. M. S. HUSSAR *by John Wetherell*—The Recollections of an Ordinary Seaman of the Royal Navy During the Napoleonic Wars.

THE NAVAL BRIGADE IN NATAL *by C. R. N. Burne*—With the Guns of H. M. S. Terrible & H. M. S. Tartar during the Boer War 1899-1900.

THE VOYAGE OF H. M. S. BOUNTY *by William Bligh*—The True Story of an 18th Century Voyage of Exploration and Mutiny.

SHIPWRECK! *by William Gilly*—The Royal Navy's Disasters at Sea 1793-1849.

KING'S CUTTERS AND SMUGGLERS: 1700-1855 *by E. Keble Chatterton*—A unique period of maritime history-from the beginning of the eighteenth to the middle of the nineteenth century when British seamen risked all to smuggle valuable goods from wool to tea and spirits from and to the Continent.

CONFEDERATE BLOCKADE RUNNER *by John Wilkinson*—The Personal Recollections of an Officer of the Confederate Navy.

NAVAL BATTLES OF THE NAPOLEONIC WARS *by W. H. Fitchett*—Cape St. Vincent, the Nile, Cadiz, Copenhagen, Trafalgar & Others.

PRISONERS OF THE RED DESERT *by R. S. Gwatkin-Williams*—The Adventures of the Crew of the Tara During the First World War.

U-BOAT WAR 1914-1918 *by James B. Connolly/Karl von Schenk*—Two Contrasting Accounts from Both Sides of the Conflict at Sea D uring the Great War.

LEONAUR

ALSO FROM LEONAUR
AVAILABLE IN SOFTCOVER OR HARDCOVER WITH DUST JACKET

IRON TIMES WITH THE GUARDS *by An O. E. (G. P. A. Fildes)*—The Experiences of an Officer of the Coldstream Guards on the Western Front During the First World War.

THE GREAT WAR IN THE MIDDLE EAST: 1 *by W. T. Massey*—The Desert Campaigns & How Jerusalem Was Won---two classic accounts in one volume.

THE GREAT WAR IN THE MIDDLE EAST: 2 *by W. T. Massey*—Allenby's Final Triumph.

SMITH-DORRIEN *by Horace Smith-Dorrien*—Isandlwhana to the Great War.

1914 *by Sir John French*—The Early Campaigns of the Great War by the British Commander.

GRENADIER *by E. R. M. Fryer*—The Recollections of an Officer of the Grenadier Guards throughout the Great War on the Western Front.

BATTLE, CAPTURE & ESCAPE *by George Pearson*—The Experiences of a Canadian Light Infantryman During the Great War.

DIGGERS AT WAR *by R. Hugh Knyvett & G. P. Cuttriss*—"Over There" With the Australians by R. Hugh Knyvett and Over the Top With the Third Australian Division by G. P. Cuttriss. Accounts of Australians During the Great War in the Middle East, at Gallipoli and on the Western Front.

HEAVY FIGHTING BEFORE US *by George Brenton Laurie*—The Letters of an Officer of the Royal Irish Rifles on the Western Front During the Great War.

THE CAMELIERS *by Oliver Hogue*—A Classic Account of the Australians of the Imperial Camel Corps During the First World War in the Middle East.

RED DUST *by Donald Black*—A Classic Account of Australian Light Horsemen in Palestine During the First World War.

THE LEAN, BROWN MEN *by Angus Buchanan*—Experiences in East Africa During the Great War with the 25th Royal Fusiliers—the Legion of Frontiersmen.

THE NIGERIAN REGIMENT IN EAST AFRICA *by W. D. Downes*—On Campaign During the Great War 1916-1918.

THE 'DIE-HARDS' IN SIBERIA *by John Ward*—With the Middlesex Regiment Against the Bolsheviks 1918-19.

LEONAUR

ALSO FROM LEONAUR
AVAILABLE IN SOFTCOVER OR HARDCOVER WITH DUST JACKET

FARAWAY CAMPAIGN *by F. James*—Experiences of an Indian Army Cavalry Officer in Persia & Russia During the Great War.

REVOLT IN THE DESERT *by T. E. Lawrence*—An account of the experiences of one remarkable British officer's war from his own perspective.

MACHINE-GUN SQUADRON *by A. M. G.*—The 20th Machine Gunners from British Yeomanry Regiments in the Middle East Campaign of the First World War.

A GUNNER'S CRUSADE *by Antony Bluett*—The Campaign in the Desert, Palestine & Syria as Experienced by the Honourable Artillery Company During the Great War .

DESPATCH RIDER *by W. H. L. Watson*—The Experiences of a British Army Motorcycle Despatch Rider During the Opening Battles of the Great War in Europe.

TIGERS ALONG THE TIGRIS *by E. J. Thompson*—The Leicestershire Regiment in Mesopotamia During the First World War.

HEARTS & DRAGONS *by Charles R. M. F. Crutwell*—The 4th Royal Berkshire Regiment in France and Italy During the Great War, 1914-1918.

INFANTRY BRIGADE: 1914 *by John Ward*—The Diary of a Commander of the 15th Infantry Brigade, 5th Division, British Army, During the Retreat from Mons.

DOING OUR 'BIT' *by Ian Hay*—Two Classic Accounts of the Men of Kitchener's 'New Army' During the Great War including *The First 100,000* & *All In It*.

AN EYE IN THE STORM *by Arthur Ruhl*—An American War Correspondent's Experiences of the First World War from the Western Front to Gallipoli-and Beyond.

STAND & FALL *by Joe Cassells*—With the Middlesex Regiment Against the Bolsheviks 1918-19.

RIFLEMAN MACGILL'S WAR *by Patrick MacGill*—A Soldier of the London Irish During the Great War in Europe including *The Amateur Army, The Red Horizon & The Great Push.*

WITH THE GUNS *by C. A. Rose & Hugh Dalton*—Two First Hand Accounts of British Gunners at War in Europe During World War 1- Three Years in France with the Guns and With the British Guns in Italy.

THE BUSH WAR DOCTOR *by Robert V. Dolbey*—The Experiences of a British Army Doctor During the East African Campaign of the First World War.

CPSIA information can be obtained at www.ICGtesting.com
Printed in the USA
LVOW060316150513

333873LV00001B/7/P